THE MEANING OF THE WAR
TO THE AMERICAS

THE MEANING OF THE WAR TO THE AMERICAS

LECTURES DELIVERED UNDER THE AUSPICES OF
THE COMMITTEE ON INTERNATIONAL RELATIONS
ON THE LOS ANGELES CAMPUS OF THE
UNIVERSITY OF CALIFORNIA, 1941

UNIVERSITY OF CALIFORNIA PRESS
BERKELEY AND LOS ANGELES
1941

UNIVERSITY OF CALIFORNIA PRESS
BERKELEY, CALIFORNIA

CAMBRIDGE UNIVERSITY PRESS
LONDON, ENGLAND

Price: Cloth, $1.50; Paper, $1.00

COPYRIGHT, 1941, BY
THE REGENTS OF THE UNIVERSITY OF CALIFORNIA

PREFACE

THE MEANING OF THE WAR TO THE AMERICAS comes by its title through a series of historic events. In the volume of lectures delivered in 1940 under the caption of *Frontiers of the Future* the Committee on International Relations began the interpretation of issues which World War II quickly pushed to the forefront of the political world stage. The intervening year, with its catastrophic events, has brought the war ever closer to the American continents, although not always so close home to the average American citizen, collegian or noncollegian. It was accordingly decided to tackle the problem of the meaning of the war boldly, frontally, in a series of addresses designed to bring into relief the variform significances of the conflict, and to attempt to reach a greater consensus, a wider "area of agreement," upon issues which already revealed deep cleavages in the American body politic. To this important task of clarification and interpretation the Committee successively summoned a philosopher, a man of science, two economists, and two men of letters, seeking by the very breadth of its coverage an ampler reading of meaning out of the cryptic handwriting on the wall of contemporary history. The pages which follow embody these interpretations.

Perhaps the most significant fact which emerges from them is the resurgence of value judgments, of positive appraisals, of ethical evaluations in dealing with the different subjects under review. Uniformly abandoning the nonchalance of the pre-War period—a nonchalance characteristic of the Era of Great Cynicism now happily past—the contributors to this volume all find meaning out of chaos and catastrophe precisely because, in an imperiled world, there is a renewed human quest for values. Whatever their specific task, the lecturers discover, each in his own discipline and at times beyond it, the things held to have positive meaning and permanent worth. This is distinctly an ascent out of the moral morass of the immediate pre-War period, with its cult of the irrational, its crass materialism, and its apparent aversion to ethical standards. The second salient characteristic in these lectures is their programmatic character. No matter from what point the approach is made, the results of scientific analysis of a given problem lead to a recommended course of action, a positive program for a way out. Nothing could be more satisfactory than this emergent triumph of dispassionate reason.

Selected to inaugurate the series, Professor Loewenberg, in the first lecture, searchingly probes the issues of the war from the standpoint of philosophy. To him the war is not an amoral, removed thing, without root causes or computable consequences. Once he touches his subject it springs into life, full of realities, significances, consequences, of vast individual and social import. There is a fair, candid, and clear-cut exposition of the isolationist thesis, followed by a fearless and devastating exposé of its fallacies. By a fundamental quest for, and return to, value judgments, Professor Loewenberg argues, will we alone be able to discover meaning in, and attach reality to, the complex of events which the second World War unfolds before our generation.

There is a reprise of this theme in the second lecture, on "Science and War," when Dean Hildebrand trenchantly de-

Preface

clares: "I cannot subscribe to the thesis that there is a dichotomy between scientific method and a set of values." To the problem of war, as faced by the scientist, Professor Hildebrand brings a rich background of experience, not only as a distinguished chemist in his own right, but also as one of the recognized pioneers in the United States Chemical Warfare Service. Boldly facing the problems of social and scientific values in relation to war, he stresses the peculiar importance of scientific method in the training of soldiers, and of scientific insight in the inventing and devising of defense against the newer enginery of war. Convinced that science and democratic society are complementary, Dean Hildebrand pleads for the cultivation of scientific aptitudes in order that the maximum of ability, inventiveness, and resourcefulness shall become available to, and come to characterize, our new citizen armies.

The two central lectures, by Professors Watkins and Wellman, are intensely concerned with very practical aspects of the situation arising out of the second World War. Viewing the terrible twists and torques of the war on the economies of the Western Hemisphere, Dean Watkins not only portrays the drastic economic effects of blockade and loss of European markets upon the other Americas, but makes concrete suggestions concerning how these stresses and strains may be overcome, in small part by unilateral, in larger part by coöperative action on the part of the United States. Indeed, "the rediscovery of the other Americas by North America" looms large as one of the most significant by-products of the war. That this unique, nonrecurring opportunity shall be intelligently used to buttress by economic measures the otherwise politically frail structure of Pan-Americanism is the plea most strongly—and rightly—urged by Dean Watkins.

Professor Wellman, in his survey of the effects of the war on the agriculture of the Western Hemisphere, follows a deeper but more specialized problem. In an irrefutable manner he shows the ruthless incidence of the war on traditional economic orbits, habitual trade routes, established markets. By a thorough breakdown of the raw data, he reveals the terrific impacts of the war's dislocations on the economies of the Americas, particularly since the fall of France. This phasal treatment, illustrating for successive periods of the war the economic consequences of the military situation, is extraordinarily illuminating. Yet Professor Wellman acurately senses the primacy of political and military considerations over commercial and even humanitarian motives in wartime, and raises, in the light of the total world situation, the all-important question of whether it would not be "the lesser of two evils ... for the United States to assist in maintaining the kind of Europe with which the South American countries as well as our own can trade without jeopardizing our security, rather than to take or underwrite their exportable surpluses." Given the raw data of economic life, even hemispheric isolation is virtually an impossibility.

In dealing with the politico-strategic aspects of the common theme, Professor Périgord subjects to a critical analysis the factors, remote and recent, on which the security of the Americas has historically been dependent, and finds that the division of Europe into opposing camps, the continued paramountcy

Preface ix

of Britain at sea, and the effective barrier of distance have combined to provide that security. Yet the virtual conquest of Europe by Hitler has removed one factor; the technological developments of modern warfare have succeeded in bridging vast distances; only British sea power stands between the Americas and conquest. It is in this perspective that Dr. Périgord treats the rapid evolution of the political measures for hemispheric defense, seeing in the development of Canadian-American and Pan-American coöperation the indispensable steps for continental security. But while registering commendable progress over tremendous obstacles, these efforts, he avows, are still incomplete and more—much more—remains to be done. Here again his is a programmatic pronouncement with respect to the unfinished tasks, now no longer primarily psychological or political, but military and economic. Thus, whether viewed from strategic, political, or economic standpoints, the final recommendations are basically the same.

The concluding lecture, by Professor Barja, brings into focus the tremendous cultural struggle that is taking place before us. As inheritors, in the Western Hemisphere, of all that is in the tradition of Western culture, there is imposed upon the peoples of the Americas the stupendous task of achieving a new cultural synthesis. For the past forty years "the old traditional relationship, in which Europe led, has gradually been changing to one in which America appears more and more as the leader, and Europe as more and more dependent on America." The two World Wars have vastly accelerated this change; in fact, "the United States has displaced Europe, the rest of the American continent being left, with respect to the United States, in a position not very dissimilar to that of Europe itself."

Analyzing the deeper causes for this displacement of Europe by America, Professor Barja finds it attributable not only to the rise of a new culture in the Western Hemisphere, but also to the decline, if not decay, of European civilization. Deeply wounded in the holocaust of 1914-1918, Europe has been unable to achieve the necessary moral convalescence or reorientation so essential to cultural survival; it has, since the first World War, been living on "borrowed time," hating its own backgrounds and ruthlessly breaking with a somber past, the traditional values of which it completely abjured.

To Latin Americans this regression has been grievous, striking at their traditional faith in the viability of European culture. The dislocation of cultural relations between the Old and New Worlds which is an inescapable consequence of the rise of totalitarianism has effected, through the mass migration of intellectuals, a final cross-fertilization of European and American cultures, although the full fruitage is yet to be harvested. Any internal cultural recovery in Europe having been postponed to the Greek calends, the interstimulation of Anglo-American and Latin American cultures—"the Americanization of the American culture"—the consequent emergence of an independent, rather nationalistic cultural system with new sets of values is in prospect. This emancipation from older European models, the gaining of autonomous momentum (albeit the imprint of the older and better Europe will be upon us), the building of a distinctive cultural mosaic in the Western Hemisphere—all these lie definitely ahead *if* totalitarian

Preface

conquest is avoided. But the building up of this culture is conditioned on the emergence of a viable economic and political order in the Western Hemisphere. Given the emergence of such an order, we may reasonably expect the return to higher standards of individual behavior and international conduct, although here, too, much remains to be done. On this note of chastened optimism, always contingent upon the victory of the Western Spirit over the rampant forces of totalitarianism, the volume closes.

In that same hope the entire series is hereby presented to the public by the Committee on International Relations.

MALBONE W. GRAHAM
Chairman

July 28, 1941

CONTENTS

	PAGE
Judgments of Fact and of Value in Relation to the War	3
By J. LOEWENBERG, Professor of Philosophy	
Science and War	37
By JOEL H. HILDEBRAND, Professor of Chemistry	
The Impact of the War on the Economic Relations of the United States and Latin America . . .	59
By GORDON S. WATKINS, Professor of Economics	
The Influence of the War on the Agriculture of the Americas	89
By HARRY R. WELLMAN, Professor of Agricultural Economics	
Politics: The Old Order and the New	117
By PAUL PÉRIGORD, Professor of French Civilization	
The War and Cultural Relations	145
By CÉSAR BARJA, Professor of Spanish	

JUDGMENTS OF FACT AND OF VALUE IN RELATION TO THE WAR

J. LOEWENBERG
PROFESSOR OF PHILOSOPHY
IN THE UNIVERSITY OF CALIFORNIA

Lecture delivered April 1, 1941

JUDGMENTS OF FACT AND OF VALUE IN RELATION TO THE WAR

IN CONSIDERING the meaning for America of the present war we must bear in mind two distinct though related judgments. One is a judgment of *fact,* and the other is a judgment of *value.* These two judgments, often confused, are not amenable to the same standard of validity. Judgments of fact have for their basis the analysis of present events in relation to their past causes and future results; judgments of value have to do with the moral significance of events, their bearing upon individual interests and social purposes. Confusion between interpretation of facts and affirmation of values may lead us astray in two directions. The analysis of events may be distorted by our desires, a distortion for which the popular name is "wishful thinking"; and the importance of events may be obscured by failure to appraise their effects upon our cherished modes of life. To understand the war in connection with the fortunes of the United States, it is necessary to discern the difference between the factual and the moral aspects of the war. The discrimination of these two aspects is the theme of the present discussion.

I

A few sample questions will illustrate the distinction between judgments of fact and judgments of value in relation to the war.

4 *The Meaning of the War*

What is the relative strength of the belligerents? Will Britain continue to rule the waves? Has superior air power the advantage over superior sea power? Will the British blockade eventually force Germany to surrender? Or can Germany succeed in her effort to blockade the British and to undermine their military resistance? Is the invasion of Britain possible? If the war develops into one of mutual attrition, which of the principal powers is likely to starve the other, not only of food but of weapons, and thus reduce it by siege? In an ultimate "war of nerves," will the morale of the British people prove more impregnable than the morale of their enemies? Will the victory of the aggressor nations constitute an immediate threat to our national security? How far should we go in averting or frustrating their designs? These are questions of fact, and concerning them experts as well as laymen have given divergent answers. There are those who say that the aggressor nations are invincible, and there are those who declare that they can be ultimately defeated. Some believe that we have little to fear from a victory of the totalitarian states, our geographic position being such as to afford us immunity from attack; others, on the contrary, advance the argument that geographic isolation is a myth, and that the invasion of the Western Hemisphere will become imminent if Britain is conquered by the dictator countries. Consequently, opinions have been at variance regarding the part we should play in the present conflict. Isolationists have tended to minimize the danger to our safety that would result from the eventual triumph of the totalitarian powers, and have counseled prudence in our policy lest we ourselves become engulfed in the war. Nonisolationists, convinced that we shall be open to aggression by a Europe under the hegemony of Germany and by an Asia under the hegemony of Japan, have advocated, in the interest of our own defense, measures short of war, and even war itself, in order to resist now, while resistance may be most effective, the challenge of the antidemocratic forces bent upon dominating the world.

Closely linked with the judgments of fact, such as those involved in the different attitudes of isolationists and nonisolationists, are judgments of value. Is the democratic way of life worth preserving and defending? Do we prefer our way to the totalitarian? Are we committed to the proposition that our constitutional and representative form of government shall remain inviolate? Do we desire to perpetuate the heritage of our civil rights and civil liberties? Are we attached to our laws and institutions which we want to perfect but not to jettison? Do we believe in the importance of our national culture in the enrichment of which all the racial stocks that compose our diverse population enjoy equality of opportunity? Are our hearts set against force and violence as arbiters in the conflict of our individual and social purposes? Do we in theory, if not in practice, cling to the view that men are not to be exploited by men in the interests of a chosen race, a chosen caste, a chosen class? These questions touch the fundamental values of Americanism, and judgments regarding them do not divide isolationists from nonisolationists. With the exception of the few who desire to refashion America to resemble Nazi Germany or Soviet Russia, our people as a whole are hostile to totalitarianism or dictatorship, adhering by tradition and sentiment to the democratic form of civilization. It is true that in their heated debates isolationists and nonisolationists are wont to impute to each other disingenuous motives. But a discussion of "motives," the pot calling the kettle black, is unprofitable. To impugn the patriotism of those who differ from us is ignoble. We may safely assume patriotic sincerity on the part of most of our isolationists and nonisolationists; both groups are inspired by the same loyalty and devotion to our national interests and values. The cleavage between them has to do with the method or policy of safeguarding these interests and values.

Indeed, without fundamental agreement on the purposes and aims of American life, the tremendous efforts we are making in behalf of national defense would not be so generally recognized as urgent and necessary. For *what* are we seeking to defend, and *against what* are we preparing to defend it?

Our theory of national defense rests first of all on the judgment that American democracy is worthy of defense. The continuity and integrity of our form of civilization must be preserved at all costs, not only for our own people, but for the benefit of all mankind, because we believe that the kind of society we have established on this continent, though not perfect, is perfectible, and perfectible in a definite direction. We have resolved to live together as free men under laws and institutions of our own making designed for our mutual protection against the tyranny of government and the anarchy of passion. In saying this we are not required to speak as apologists for things as they are. There is, alas, much in our present order which justifies condemnation. Our society is far from ideal. But as long as the democratic framework of our society remains unimpaired, our government being a government resting on the consent of the governed, criticism of the evils from which we suffer is legitimate, and their correction or reform is not precluded by the concerted action of our people. We have the instrumentalities under our Constitution to produce changes in the economic and social conditions of our national life in accordance with our collective conceptions of right and justice. The hope of a more humane order, though deferred for lack of social thought and wisdom, is deeply embedded in a democratic state in which the general will has for its accepted vehicle the verdict of the majority. Such hope is denied to those who live under a totalitarian regime in complete servitude to the absolute state and in blind obedience to its despotic leaders. The moral argument for defending American democracy draws its support from the faith of our people in their ideals and aspirations, and from their hope of an enlightened society that will make possible for its members greater participation in the material and spiritual fruits of human intelligence and industry. In the absence of this pervasive faith and hope in democracy the need for its defense could be made neither convincing nor effective.

Why democracy should be defended is thus not a matter of controversy if we believe as we do that a regimented life, such as is lived by those in totalitarian states, is not the good life. The conception of a free society, not dominated by hate and fear, is America's heritage and promise, and we are now arming to resist, by force if necessary, any challenge to our democratic state, developed in the course of our history, and susceptible of improvement as a more adequate instrument of human civilization. Although the need of defending the values embodied in American democracy is almost axiomatic, *how* to defend them, and under what conditions—this is indeed a subject of dispute.

For the theory of national defense depends not only on the judgment that America is worth defending but also on the appraisal of present and future events in relation to our interests and security. Such appraisal is a judgment of facts, facts intricate and multitudinous, and no man can lay claim to certain or complete knowledge of them. A judgment of what may or might confront us, and against which we should be prepared, is at best only plausible or probable. No wonder there has been divided counsel among us with respect to the nature and extent of our preparedness.

Should our defense be planned on the assumption that the aggressor nations would not win the war, or, if victorious, would be too sated or too exhausted to attack us in the near future? Or should we be guided by the hypothesis that the enemies of democracy, after conquering the powers opposed to them, would be able to launch a formidable assault on this hemisphere? Should we aid England and her allies without weakening our own strength, on the supposition that it is too late for such aid to be decisive; or should we intervene in the struggle now, with all the resources at our command, the chances of defeating the aggressors being propitious in proportion as the British still resist? Must we keep out of the war lest by entering it we might destroy democracy at home

Loewenberg: Judgments

in the process of making it safe for the world; or would our participation in the conflict, while involving a temporary suspension of our democratic ways, prevent the rise of the "new order" in Europe and Asia against which we should have to fight in the end on unequal terms? To these questions we have heard divergent answers, all based upon judgments of fact, the validity of which cannot be said to enjoy certainty but only varying degrees of probability.

I have attempted to distinguish the judgments of value from the judgments of fact, underlying our theory of national defense, in order to clarify the crucial issues with which we are faced. The two kinds of judgment are not on the same plane of thought. The difference between them, to express it succinctly, is the difference between the *reasons* for national defense and the *causes* of national defense. The reasons have their root in the general and firm resolve of our people that our form of government, and the mode of life to which it is ancillary, shall not, in Lincoln's phrase, "perish from the earth." The causes hinge upon specific and fluctuating events, as they occur or might occur, threatening the security of our national existence. Concerning the reasons for defending America there must be relative unanimity and certainty, since without such unanimity and certainty our allegiance would not be wholehearted and our determination not steadfast. But what particular events, in the present or the future, we should regard as causes of danger to our safety, to be met by definite plans of action—this is a debatable question and one entailing a calculus of probabilities. I shall return later to the compelling reasons for the defense of America. But first let me speak of the causes of our defense. About the effects of these causes upon the destiny of our national life experts and laymen entertain different hypotheses.

II

The effects of causes, whether proximate or remote, are matters of calculation. No nation is safe unless those responsible for shaping its policy can compute in advance, with a fair degree of adequacy, the chances of danger threatening its independent existence. The fate of miscalculation, as history has abundantly shown, is defeat and destruction. The countries now conquered by the Nazis owe their tragic plight to mistaken judgments of fact regarding Germany's power and her intention to use that power for purposes of aggression. The handwriting on the wall, legible alas! only with our present "hindsight," should have been seen or read by the European governments charged with the task of preparing their respective nations for the impending and inevitable struggle. Instead, they acquiesced in Germany's vast rearmament, in the violation of her treaties, in her annexation of Austria and Czechoslovakia. They suffered the Nazis to go from strength to strength, relying upon Hitler's word that each of his territorial claims would be his last. They hoped, credulous of Nazi propaganda against communism, that Germany's might would be turned in the direction of Soviet Russia. To preserve peace in Europe, "peace in our time," they embarked upon a policy of appeasement. And when Germany at last moved into Poland, with her new method of warfare made manifest to all the military experts of the world, the governments of Europe failed signally to gauge the striking power of her weapons and the nature of her stratagems and tactics. France continued to pin her faith upon the Maginot Line as an impregnable barricade. England continued to put her trust in her navy as a permanent insurance against invasion. And the smaller countries continued to follow a course of scrupulous neutrality, confiding in German promises of friendship and nonaggression. Most of the calculations made by the nations in fear of Germany's gathering force and sinister design have proved to be miscalculations. As a consequence, Germany is in virtual control of continental Europe, and the hope to keep "Hitlerism," with all that the term implies, from becoming finally triumphant, now centers in Britain's heroic effort.

The wisdom gained from a retrospective view of causes that might have been checked or deflected is of little practical value unless such wisdom sharpens our foresight and determines our present plans of action. It is vain to speculate what would have happened if the statesmen of Europe had taken seriously Hitler's *Mein Kampf,* and had intervened, when intervention was feasible, to block in its early stages the path of Germany's conquest, a path so clearly adumbrated in that document. But it is not idle to speculate regarding Germany's future plans for a "new order" and their effect upon our national safety. Indeed, it is this projected "new order," projected by Germany in concert with her allies and satellites, which dictates our present policy and our present endeavor.

Our great undertakings, both military and industrial, have a definite direction. We are mobilizing all our resources to meet an eventual challenge to our security from particular powers. We are obviously not marshaling our forces to resist aggression from China or Britain. The only two nations against whose possible courses of action we are preparing are Japan and Germany. No other nations are likely to attack us. Japan alone is not formidable enough to threaten us. We have to reckon with Japan only as an ally of a victorious Germany. It is from a future triumphant Germany, with the British fleet no longer affording us protection, that the menace to our national life may be ultimately expected. Against this contingency, and against no other, we are now making our supreme effort in national defense.

It is instructive to recall that the acceleration in the tempo of our national defense has been the result of the successive and successful conquests of Germany. Before Hitler marched into Poland, and during the era of appeasement, there was in this country little popular support for military preparedness. The belief was general that a European war was improbable, and would not, if it came, gravely affect our national security. Even after the war broke out, and during the early stages when it was shortsightedly described as "phony," we felt safe from its repercussions, depending upon legal "neutrality" to keep us immune. It is only since the invasion by Germany of Holland and Belgium that our program of defense began to take shape. And it is only after the collapse of France, Britain alone remaining to bear the brunt of the struggle, that our program of defense acquired its present momentum, involving conscription of men and expansion of industry, with necessary aid to England forming an integral part of it.

Thus, if this is not too simplified a statement, the eventual challenge to us and to our hemisphere by a victorious Germany bent upon world conquest is the primary cause of our present policy and action. We are not certain how the war will end; nor are we certain, assuming it to end in Germany's favor, whether we shall be subject to attack and in what form. Certainty regarding future events is precluded. In preparing to meet them we can only be guided by a calculus of probabilities.

But no such calculus, however expert and authoritative, is an adequate basis on which to stake the fortunes of our country. To be guided merely by the probable occurrence or nonoccurrence of particular events is to take a gambler's chance; and such a gambler's chance is precisely what the governments of Europe may be said to have taken, before and since the outbreak of the war, in their judgments of fact concerning Germany's power and purpose. Confusing the impossible with the seemingly improbable, they eliminated from their calculations the likelihood of many a contingency—for example, the contingency of the defeat of France in a few weeks by the same method of warfare that proved so effective in Poland. But the improbable is never the impossible, and no nation can afford to risk its destiny on the hazard that events will not occur because the likelihood of their occurrence may now be deemed to have a very low ratio. Safety lies in providing against the low as well as against the high ratio of probability, for the future may reverse our present balancing of chances. In other words, judgments of *probability* are not enough; in matters of national policy and action, a government must take into its reckoning judgments of genuine *possibility*.

14 *The Meaning of the War*

Suppose we give a low rating to the probability of the judgment, a judgment entertained by many people, that Germany, after defeating Britain, could invade this hemisphere and successfully attack this country. Make this rating very low, and say that the chances are in the ratio of 20 to 80. Of course, a numerical computation so precise is here precluded. Responsible experts, taking into account the many uncertain and variable factors that enter into a situation of such great complexity, would hesitate to deliver themselves of any judgment laying claim to mathematical validity. But assuming that the experts could agree on a numerical statement of this kind, what should our policy be in relation to it? Should we take a gambler's chance and wager, in accordance with present estimates, on the more rather than on the less probable contingencies that may occur in the future? In the ordinary affairs of life, when what is at stake does not touch our deepest interests and values, we are prone to risk possible loss in the face of a greater likelihood of gain. We are willing to take a chance when loss as a result of miscalculation is loss of what is relatively unimportant. But the gambler who throws away his life or his home in consequence of a mistaken forecast of events is not the exemplar of sanity or wisdom; and a government gambling on the outcome of things as if it were playing dice is downright criminal. Although the forecast of any future contingency may turn out to be erroneous, a government intent upon the safety of its nation must prepare for the worst, however low in the scale of probability. As far as our own national security is concerned, nothing could be worse than a possible victory of Germany over Britain, and a possible subsequent assault upon this hemisphere. If this is possible at all—and few there are who can say with assurance that it is not,—the policy of our government is thus clearly indicated: it cannot ignore or neglect the chance that what now seems but possible may become increasingly probable. Of what transpires at present on the world stage no man is omniscient enough to foretell with certainty the direction and the effect.

III

Yet there are many citizens in this country, citizens whose patriotism is above suspicion, who wish our government to take a gambler's chance in relation to our future security. These citizens, some representatives in the Congress of the United States and some leaders of opinion outside the Congress, have told us, in accordance with their judgments of fact, not what may happen but what will happen as a result of our foreign policy. They have told us that this policy will involve this country in war, will deplete our own defenses by giving excessive aid to Britain, will lead to dictatorship here while supporting the cause of democracy abroad. These things, they have said, will happen if we acquiesce in the course of action charted by the Administration. And they have offered these judgments not as possible or as probable, but as certain.

In the light of these judgments, what should we do then? What should be the alternative policy?

The alternative policy has been that of isolationism. According to the advocates of the many variants of isolationism—some prefer to call their view nonintervention—our policy should be a policy of "America First." Such a policy should be determined by our own interests, which are not those of other nations. The struggle between Britain and her enemies, it is asserted, is a struggle for power, a struggle in which we have no concern and from which therefore we should remain aloof. Whatever the outcome of this struggle, our own safety will not be affected by it. Opposed on moral grounds to totalitarianism, isolationists are equally revolted by British imperialism. We should indeed be prepared for defense, but for defense of our continent, and even of our hemisphere, *if* and *when* we are actually attacked or invaded. Aid to Britain, since this is the policy to which we are now committed, should not reduce the effectiveness of such defensive weapons as might be needed for our own use. Whether we shall ever be required to employ our armed forces to repel an enemy is problematic. Our geographic position insures us against attack, whether by air or sea; and should such attack, which isolationists consider unlikely, be attempted, our ability to defeat it may be taken for granted if our national defense is planned for that purpose and for that purpose alone. Fear of Germany and her partners is due to "hysteria" fostered by the propaganda of "warmongers." What we have to fear is the menace to our liberties by the belligerent policy of the Administration. We are in danger of repeating the disastrous crusade of the last war "to make the world safe for democracy." Our first and paramount duty is to make democracy secure in our own land. This can be achieved by keeping out of a foreign struggle for power and by attending strictly to those domestic problems the solution of which will preserve and improve the American way of life.

This, I think, is a fair though condensed statement of the isolationist attitude. For this attitude there are two major arguments. One is a moral argument, the other a factual one. The moral argument for isolationism turns upon the interpretation of the present struggle as a struggle for power in the outcome of which the cause of democracy is not involved. The survival of the British Empire is not essential to that cause, for imperialism and democracy are ultimately incompatible. To "underwrite" a British victory by our participation in the conflict is to perpetuate an imperialism which owes its existence and expansion to past conquests, an imperialism no less odious than the German kind seeking to supplant it by the same methods of aggression. This is not a war for universal liberty and justice. It is a war between two world powers, one fighting to preserve its imperialist rule and the other to replace it, and in such a war we should be neutral. There is little to choose between Britannia and Germania as mistress over a large surface of the earth. That this is an imperialist war, we may observe in passing, has been the official communist view. What irony to find this view reiterated by those committed to the defense of capitalism! Moral justification of the isolationist position requires that Britain and Germany be tarred with the same brush, a feat that can be accomplished only by accentuating the evils of one imperialism and by blurring those of the other.

Now one need not be an Anglophile to reject the isolationist thesis that British imperial policy is as inimical to the cause of democracy as the imperial policy of the Nazis would be if they succeeded in establishing their "new order." One consideration is here decisive. British imperial policy is fixed by a Parliament of freely chosen representatives, and there is hope for those who suffer from British misrule under a government responsible and responsive to the demands of public opinion, voiced without constraint in an uncensored press and through uncontrolled elections. Such public opinion may be instrumental, for example, in satisfying India's aspiration for dominion status. We must not forget that the Irish Free State owes its being to an act of Parliament. Where there is parliamentary life, sustained by free speech and free associations and in turn sustaining them, there is always hope for change and amelioration of existing conditions. The minority of today may become the majority of tomorrow. A reactionary government may be succeeded by a liberal one. The British Empire, directed by a country whose government embodies the will of a majority of the electorate, can thus not be placed on the same moral plane as an empire ruled by a dictator nation.

For the imperial policy of a dictator nation is determined by the despotic masters of it governing by force and terror. There is no consensus of public opinion to sanction such a policy. There is no minority, capable of becoming the majority, exercising the prerogative of "loyal opposition." All opposition is not only disloyal but treasonable, headed for the concentration camp or the executioner's axe. What the Nazis exact is absolute servitude to the state, its powers and glory being exalted as the highest good. Man exists to serve the state, not the state to serve man, and the state comprehends the whole of life. All human activities are under its direction and control. The interests of the state are supreme, defining the value of men's thoughts and men's aspirations. In the promotion of these interests, and these interests alone, lies the standard of truth, goodness, and beauty. Dictatorship is unlimited, extending not only to the sphere of politics and economics, but also to religion, art, science, and philosophy. The term "totalitarian" for this form of dictatorship is well chosen: it means complete and unconditional domination by a single and central authority of all belief and all action. Such is the totalitarianism which is the inexorable lot of nations and peoples fated for hegemony by the master-state of Nazi Germany. Suppose, for instance, British rule of India were replaced by Nazi rule. What would be her destiny? Indian hope for self-government, however deferred at present, would become extinct, just as extinct as the hope for independence of all other peoples now conquered—the Scandinavian, the Balkan, the Polish, the Dutch, the Belgian, the French—if condemned to live under Nazi tyranny in a new imperial system.

So, even if the war be looked upon as a struggle for empire, which is a superficial view of it, German imperialism would spell the doom of democracy everywhere. British imperialism, though it be painted in colors of the darkest hue, may delay but does not preclude the liberation of those under its rule, for it is based on parliamentarism, and parliamentarism, unlike totalitarianism, cannot permanently corrode human faith in reason and human passion for justice.

The moral argument for isolationism that democracy has nothing at stake in the supposititious struggle for empire, British imperialism being as iniquitous as German imperialism, is thus without validity and can carry no conviction for those who regard British political philosophy as cognate with our own. Totalitarianism is not an alternative, but the very antithesis, of parliamentarism. The worst of Tories are preferable to the best of Nazis. There is always the possibility of redress from the policies of Tories, since their power is open to overt challenge by an electorate having at its disposal free organs of expression and association; but from the implacable will of Nazis to strike at the heart of democracy, and to "liquidate" it everywhere, root and branch, there is no deliverance save to meet force with force. British imperialism is susceptible of reform by democratic thought and action; Nazi imperialism, committed as it is to the destruction of human rights and liberties, could only be defeated in its revolutionary design by counterrevolution within or by war from without. The failure to recognize totalitarianism for what it is, namely, an incendiary revolution, global in scope, is a failure of singular gravity. The moral judgment that there is no difference between British and German imperialism is a moral misjudgment that augurs ill for the cause of democracy.

The moral misjudgment of isolationists is bewildering enough. More bewildering is the factual argument for their isolationism. Here we are faced with contradictory statements, depending upon whether we listen to those who are pessimistic about the survival of the British Empire or to those who are optimistic about it.

The pessimists view Britain's defeat as a foregone conclusion. We shall only squander the resources needed for our own defense, they contend, if our aid to England is too prodigal. Our aid now will be either too late or too insufficient to avert the inevitable. This is essentially the German and the Italian thesis, to which some of our isolationists have openly subscribed. Why not be "realistic"? Let us accept the facts as they are. Let us mind our own business, which is to make ourselves so strong that no power or combination of powers would dare attack us. This, of course, rests on the sanguine assumption that we shall have time, after the expected German victory, to attain this requisite strength—a two-ocean navy, a mechanized army, a formidable air force, an economy adequate to cope with that of a United Europe under Nazi regimentation.

The optimists consider as remote, if not negligible, the danger of German aggression on this continent or hemisphere. They discount the notion of England's imminent defeat, pointing to the difficult, not to say impossible, task of invading the British Isles. If the Nazi hosts find the stretch of water separating them from England such an impassable barrier, how fantastic the likelihood of their crossing the Atlantic Ocean! We should be safe from invasion for a long time, long enough to marshal all our forces of resistance, if invasion were to be attempted in the event of England's improbable collapse or surrender. Yes, improbable, if we consider her vast imperial resources, her mighty army, her invincible navy, her increasing air force, the indomitable spirit of her people. The British empire is tougher than we have been led to believe; it is premature, therefore, to lament its demise. Our policy should thus be one of prudence, aiming at conserving and perfecting our own strength without weakening it by lavish aid to England. Such aid should be limited to stiffening her resistance and not to "underwriting" her victory. By a cautious limitation of our aid we shall avoid being drawn into the conflict, and we may be instrumental in bringing about a "negotiated peace." This is not our war, and by remaining aloof from it we shall shorten its duration. A stalemate in the struggle would be more consonant with our national interests than a decisive victory for one of the belligerents. Complete economic disintegration and bankruptcy of Europe could be averted only by the conclusion of an early peace, followed by a speedy restoration of the normal processes of international trade and commerce. Upon the conclusion of an early peace our own prosperity ultimately depends. In a word, interventionism would prolong the war, terminating in the ruin of both victor and vanquished; noninterventionism might hasten its end, and the sooner the war is ended, the better for us and for the world.

Thus those who are pessimistic about England's chances to survive have argued that total aid to her is now too late to be effective; those who are optimistic about these chances have argued for the withholding of total aid because it is not necessary. But these contradictory factual judgments point to the same conviction, namely, that our own immediate security is not involved in the outcome of the struggle. Isolationists, whether despairing or sanguine regarding the survival of the British Empire, entertain no doubt about our own survival, if our defense is planned merely to repel a direct attack upon our continent or hemisphere, an attack which they consider neither likely nor imminent. It would have been wiser, they hold, if we had not departed from a policy of strict neutrality, and they have consistently opposed and decried every new departure from it as a perilous step nearer the brink of war. Although it is too late for neutrality, increasing aid to Britain being incompatible with it, it is not too late for nonbelligerency.

It is important to note that the factual argument for isolationism is not founded upon knowledge but upon belief. Knowledge of past and present events, which forms the only basis for prediction, is difficult enough, but no man can claim to have knowledge of future events unless he claims to be omniscient and infallible. With respect to the future all our judgments are judgments of belief. Do isolationists *know* whether England will survive or not? Do they *know* that the destruction of her empire will not constitute an immediate danger to the security of the United States? Their statements have no other validity than that pertaining to a calculus of probabilities, a calculus which can never be mathematical in precision or accuracy, and one which the future may prove to be altogether erroneous. We must not forget that the calculations of chances which guided the European statesmen prior to Munich and thereafter were miscalculations most tragic in their consequences. Upon a calculus of contingencies, which future events may likewise invalidate, American isolationists have been disposed to stake our national safety and destiny. They have been willing, as I have said, to take a gambler's chance. Any belief about the future as a guide to present action involves serious hazards. But the policy of isolationism entails a grave risk not precluded by any calculus of probabilities: it is the risk of saddling our nation with the Herculean task of having to fight in the future, alone and against heavy odds, a combination of totalitarian powers that may have at their disposal military resources exceeding our own, and economic weapons more potent than ours. Only by discounting this risk could isolationism be justified.

IV

But this risk cannot be discounted. To provide against incurring it is the aim of the President's foreign policy, the policy of turning this country into an "arsenal of democracy," and of lending or leasing to England such instruments of warfare as she may need to resist and ultimately to defeat Germany, the premise being that a Nazi triumph would constitute a menace to our own national security. Of the shape of things to come neither isolationists nor nonisolationists possess preternatural knowledge. The clash between them is a clash of belief. But the belief directing the policy of the Administration seems more plausible in the light of past and present events. Moreover, determined action upon this belief may render impossible what now seems probable, namely, a future attack upon us by the combined forces of totalitarian powers. No man concerned with his individual security can afford to let things take their course, trusting to luck that they will not work to his disadvantage. Preventive medicine, to take one example out of many, would be foolish if we could not guard against *manifest* dangers to our health. We do not remain passive in the presence of such dangers; we intervene to avert them either by checking the effects of actual causes or by bringing into play the action of new causes. A nation, if it is to survive, must proceed in a similar manner. To await a possible attack, confident that we shall be able to resist it, is like waiting for the development of a cancer, hoping for its successful removal by a later surgical operation. As it is part of individual wisdom to prevent the growth of a cancer in its incipient stages, so it is part of national wisdom not to allow a situation to attain its maximum peril. Safety lies in frustrating its baneful influence while the peril is still inchoate.

The foreign policy of our national Administration is thus the policy of preventive action. It rests on the diagnosis of totalitarianism as a cancerous growth in the world which will destroy democracy everywhere unless its spread is now checked and its source ultimately removed. And this farsighted policy is a compound of pessimism and optimism.

The pessimistic part of it is justified by a serious consideration of two possible eventualities, one that without our full and sustained assistance England *may* be defeated, and the other that after England's defeat aggression upon us *may* be attempted before we are adequately prepared to meet it. These two possibilities, one conditioning the other, are not imaginary, and in taking cognizance of them the Administration is not lulling us into a false security based upon a gambler's attitude that because the odds are against the occurrence of certain events it is safe to bet on their nonoccurrence. A nation must prepare for any calamity that may befall it. The worst calamity for us would be England's possible collapse, her navy in Germany's possession, and her empire under direct or indirect Nazi control. This might happen. And because it might happen we are resolved that it shall not happen. This resolution governs our policy of complete aid to Britain. The Lease-Lend Law embodying this policy can be defended on no other ground.

But this policy of preventive action has an optimistic aspect, namely, that the calamity mentioned can be averted, for we are rich in potential resources and strong in industrial capacity. We are now engaged in the effort to convert the expression, "an arsenal of democracy," from a figure of speech into a stark reality. By supplying aid to Britain, without stint and on an ever-increasing scale, the enemy could be halted in his tracks and finally overcome. But we must have a united will to believe that this could be done, for such a will is not the least factor in computing the chances of success. The resolute will to resist and to win has continued unabatedly to animate the British people in their unequal struggle against a ruthless conqueror; our mounting support, both material and moral, should renew and rekindle its strength. And in proportion as the morale of the British waxes, that of their enemy should wane. This view can obviously not be justified by an appeal to certainty; the appeal here is to probability, but to a probability stronger than that upon which the opposition has relied for a policy of inaction or of such action as is hesitant and timorous. The Administration's policy of preventive action, if carried out with inflexible determination, contains the only promise and hope of effectively thwarting and subduing the power of Nazi Germany.

Passage by the Congress of the United States of the Lease-Lend Bill has irrevocably committed our nation to nonisolationism in the present conflict. It is the general will of the people, as expressed through the democratic processes and methods of our representative form of government, that the President pursue with vigor his policy of preventive action. This policy of preventive action has so far been construed as one "short of war." To what extent does this policy incur the risk of war? Future events alone can dictate our future policy. There is no policy aiming to safeguard our national existence that can altogether eliminate the risk of war. But a policy of inaction, it may be argued and argued cogently, is fraught with dangers far greater than a policy of preventive action. I must allude again to the analogy with medicine. There is always the possibility that one may succumb to a disease, no matter what measures are taken to check its advance. But this is no argument in favor of passivity and acquiescence. Recovery is rendered more probable by active prevention than by permitting the disease to run its inevitable course.

Totalitarianism is a deadly disease, and to assist by all the means in our power those fighting to eradicate it from the world is now the fixed purpose of the United States. This purpose forms an integral part of our national defense, and rightly so, our chief aim being to protect ourselves by protecting democratic civilization from a fatal virus. We have resolved that the present acute phase of barbarism must not be allowed to become chronic. The history of this new barbarism has shown that no nation can acquire immunity from its eruptive virulence either by neutrality or by appeasement. If democratic civilization is to survive, the malignant tumor threatening to destroy it must be extirpated. This, and only this, is the moral justification of our national effort to hinder at whatever cost a Nazi victory.

The Meaning of the War

v

The reason for defending America is thus clear and unambiguous. It rests on the belief, for which there is sufficient factual evidence, that democracy cannot survive unless a new epidemic of barbarism is prevented from spreading over the entire world. But does democracy deserve to survive? This is a moral question, and the answer to it in the affirmative cannot be made convincing unless the assumption is valid that democracy, though not perfect, is a perfectible instrument or vehicle in behalf of the civilized values of life. How valid is the assumption?

Viewed in historical perspective, the theory of democracy is a vindication of liberty, in the sense defined by Rousseau, as "obedience to law that the individual freely accepts for himself." The ideal synthesis of law and liberty is the distinguishing mark of the democratic state. Contrasted with a totalitarian state, the democratic state is not man's master, but his servant; it is the political organ and the legal custodian of his inalienable right to live the life of an autonomous human being not in servitude to other men. The conception of a democratic state, if it is to function as such an organ or custodian, presupposes a general will on the part of its constituent citizens to surrender private claims and counterclaims, and to submit to a representative voice and agency of the public good. Fundamental to the democratic state is the voluntary coöperation of its members, a coöperation that may be accorded or withheld, for its authority is not self-assumed but freely conceded by a people for the governance of their common life. The democratic state has no anchor save in the conviction that, if men must live together, the exemplary way of living together is by mutual respect, sympathy, and tolerance, free from coercion on individual opinion, taste, and conscience. If democracy is but a synonym for a mechanism in which private rights and private liberties are in an unstable equilibrium, it is hardly worth defending. Its defense is intelligible only on the view that democracy is a spiritual symbol of a communal life, kindled by joint aspirations and embodied in institutions sustained by a consensus of persuasions. The line between a democratic state and a totalitarian one remains indelible so long as allegiance to our communal ends is not exacted by external compulsion. Loyalty to the democratic state is not extorted loyalty, but solicited loyalty. The appeal is ultimately to intelligence, an appeal that will not be heeded wholeheartedly if the ends of democracy cannot be shown to be coterminous with those of civilization itself. Intellectual and moral commitment to the ideals of a democratic society is an indispensable condition of its existence and survival. When this commitment ceases to be a vital force in the mentality and character of a people, democracy becomes the fragile shell of a spiritless thing. The American people, I think, are deeply committed to the ideals of a democratic society, especially now when their mode of life, in spite of its flaws and imperfections, is contrasted with the mode of life under fanatic and megalomaniac dictators.

In the last analysis, the moral justification of democracy depends upon the cogency of the argument that democracy alone affords the possibility of a humane way of life. The relief of man's estate, a crying need in the economic sphere, is not precluded in a society amenable to "self-government." However harsh the judgments one passes on those who wield power in our capitalistic economy, such power is subject to restraint and regulation by the democratic process. The laws under which our economy operates are laws made by the freely elected representatives of a people enjoying civil rights and liberties. An electorate exercising these rights and liberties may, through a change of representatives, change the economic conditions of the social order. This view, I am aware, will be rejected as incredibly naïve by minds subtler or more cynical than mine. But I invite such minds to consider the alternative regime, that of totalitarianism, under which all men must surrender all freedom, for the glory and the power of the master-state or the master-race, in exchange for a dictated and precarious security. Democracy is an elastic framework and not a closed system, and within that framework men have the means to effect reform of the maladjustments in their social existence. But the possession of these means does not guarantee their adequate employment. The principles of democracy cannot be indicted because men do not use them efficiently to achieve social improvement or reconstruction. Failure to take full advantage of democratic opportunities is due to men's ignorance of their own good, to their blindness to their own ideals, to their callous deflection from their professed standards. To disparage human ineptitude to realize the principles of democracy is no disparagement of the principles themselves.

Is this ineptitude corrigible by education? Many have

thought so. But democracy can be defended as a framework of a humane life, and not as a system for the total regimentation of life, so long as education does not become a specific function of statecraft. Free education, in the sense of keeping open the channels of inquiry and criticism, is both the base and the summit of civilization, and curtailment of educational freedom by the state is a deliberate blockade of intelligence and imagination to the unhampered exercise of which civilization owes its efflorescence. Untrammeled liberty of teaching and learning is a necessary condition of democracy as a framework coextensive with that of civilization. Here perhaps lies the deepest contrast between democracy and totalitarianism.

In dictator countries the conception of a free mind is a noxious weed to be uprooted. The regimentation of the total life of society demands the regimentation of the souls and minds of men, and for the accomplishment of this end all the educational forces of the state are marshaled and mobilized. In education as thus conceived, teaching becomes indoctrination and learning compliance. The most adequate symbol for this educational theory and practice is the "straitjacket": men's beliefs and loyalties must be pressed into Procrustean molds. The formation of minds in prescribed directions is an indispensable condition for the kind of society the leaders of totalitarian states seek to establish and to perpetuate. What they exact from all members of society is blind worship and unquestioning obedience. Free inquiry and free criticism being inimical to such a society, the art of education must thus be assiduously devoted to the inculcation of fanaticism and idolatry, fanaticism of belief in the dogmas of its leaders, and idolatry towards the tribe or the state. It is indeed necessary to train individuals for efficient service, each in accordance with his particular talent or capacity; but more fundamental is their "cultural" training, training in zealous devotion to the chauvinistic cult of a chosen people, mystic faith in the infallibility of their rulers, passionate conviction in the grandeur of their common destiny, clannish hatred of nations and classes opposed to their revolutionary cause. The totalitarian system of education is a powerful weapon designed for disciplining minds into absolute submission to the supreme and unchecked will of the state.

The democracy of our education, with all its failures and blunders, is a precious heritage, and those who impugn it are openly or secretly bent upon the regimentation of minds in behalf of ideas and beliefs alien to the democratic state. For only in the democratic state, within the framework of which the cultivation of free and independent minds remains inviolable, can the labor of civilization be performed. But such labor must be understood as labor devoted to the pursuit of knowledge and beauty and to the attainment of justice and love. Democracy alone provides the opportunity for the unhindered development of science and philosophy, for the unconstrained creation of art, for the uncontrolled expression of moral and religious persuasions. The ultimate test of civilization must be in terms of those universal interests that unite men in a common humanity, decivilizing interests being such as insulate men from each other by impassable barriers of race or nation. Civilization is at once a summary and a vindication of whatever is humane in human life; it is a name for mankind's incessant aspiration and effort to relinquish the state of nature, a state marked by the absence of sanity, dignity, and solidarity. Viewed thus, the ideal of democracy is synonymous with the ideal of civilization. Democracy in action is an approximation to its ideal if it cherishes the love of peace instead of glorifying war, if it fosters reason and understanding rather than hatred and fear, if it cultivates voluntary coöperation among men and not sullen submissiveness or abject servility. In a word, democracy in action, though but an imperfect embodiment of its own ideal, draws its nutriment from an enduring faith and a living hope, faith in man's latent humanity, and hope in the release of his better nature for the tasks of enriching and enhancing the life of the spirit, the life of disinterested knowledge, creative imagination, generous feeling, pervasive charity.

The statement that the defense of democracy involves the defense of civilization itself is thus no hyperbole. The higher values of civilization, those embodied in art, science, religion, and philosophy, can come to fruition only within the framework of a democratic society in which human intelligence is free and autonomous. Of such a democratic society in the making, dedicated to the advancement of civilization as the repository of the faith and the hope of our common humanity, America has always been the determined champion. Ours is still "the promised land," not yet flowing with milk and honey, but destined to preserve and to perpetuate the heritage of Western culture now threatened by a new and fanatical barbarism.

The Meaning of the War

That totalitarianism is a recrudescence of barbarism, a return, as it were, to a state of nature as described by Hobbes, has become increasingly apparent. Totalitarianism is the exaltation of the principle of irrationality. It is the incarnation of brute force, tribal cruelty, and primitive violence. It seeks to substitute the reign of terror for the rule of reason, and under such a reign, if it became universal, the fairest fruits of the human spirit would wither and decay. Totalitarianism, if triumphant, would suspend everywhere free science, free philosophy, free art, free worship, free speech, free assembly, free government, free labor. All the rights of man, gradually established in the course of time, would disappear from the face of the earth. What a Nazi victory portends is a dark age for mankind, darker perhaps than any recorded in human history.

Hitler has characterized the war as a war between "two worlds." He is right. To acquiesce in his victorious march is to acquiesce in his world of human slavery. Shall it be his world or shall it be our world? This is the supreme issue of the present crisis.

SCIENCE AND WAR

JOEL H. HILDEBRAND
PROFESSOR OF CHEMISTRY
IN THE UNIVERSITY OF CALIFORNIA

Lecture delivered April 8, 1941

SCIENCE AND WAR

THE SCIENTIST of today is the target of two conflicting criticisms. Some expect him to keep within professional bounds and not assume to deal with matters beyond his own proper scientific sphere. Others criticize him for failing to give due heed to the effect of his scientific discoveries upon his fellow men. He is therefore urged with increasing insistence to prove himself a human being as well as a scientist. I must confess to a good deal of sympathy with the latter point of view, while reserving at the same time a critical attitude toward those scientists who transgress the boundaries of their scientific competence without the humility appropriate when expressing lay opinions. The topic assigned to me removes me, or rather one foot, from the pedestal of professional competence and makes me subject to criticism by members of my audience who may be equally qualified to form judgments regarding certain items of this address. The other foot will, however, remain on the pedestal, composed of an unusual mixture of scientific, engineering, and military experience. I wish to be perfectly frank about the double nature of my support, in order to be free to express certain personal convictions without obscuring their merits by resentment over unwarranted claims to authority.

In dealing with so momentous a topic as war, it would hardly be honest even for a scientist to pretend to hide some of his extrascientific reactions. However, I see no reason why he should hesitate to express them, particularly when they seem to involve certain elements of sound analysis which are features of the scientific method. I cannot subscribe to the thesis that there is a dichotomy between scientific method and a set of values. If natural science per se ignores values, the natural scientist need not, for everything he does with science touches values in some way. Judgments regarding values are affected by the long-term results of alternative sets of values, and these are usually to be determined by the aid of scientific studies. I do not believe it to be scientific to be altogether dispassionate regarding the possible effects of the present world situation either upon science or upon scientists and laymen. The universities of the dwindling democratic world cannot be blind to a situation fraught with such dire possibilities. Truth and falsehood are today not playing chess with each other, but are fighting to the death. I for one cannot view the struggle from the sidelines.

War and social values.—The coupling of science and war in my topic recalls a view expressed by some that science should be held responsible for war. This is on a par with the resentment of a child against the door on which he bumps his head. It completely overlooks the fact that war long antedated any organized science. If applied with complete logic, this view would deprive us of all the peaceful fruits of science merely because some of them can also be adapted to dealing death and destruction. We should have to throw them away one by one, and finally, when we had reverted to barbarism, the problem would not even then have been solved, for we would have to accuse trees of fomenting war because we could still fight with wooden clubs.

There is no greater evidence of moral immaturity than hunting scapegoats for one's own shortcomings. It is bad enough to unload responsibility upon other persons. It is incredibly silly to dump it onto impersonal factors. Science, like war or printing or money, is a means adaptable to a variety of ends. The moral responsibility for these ends, whether good or bad, rests not upon the means but upon the men who employ them. Wars have been fought over religion; should we therefore attempt to abolish religion?

I should like to make it perfectly clear that I do not regard the use of science for war as necessarily a prostitution of science. It depends on what one is fighting for. War is not a game that two parties agree to play together for their mutual satisfaction. It is usually forced by aggression, and one party chooses it as the lesser of two great evils. There are those who deny this, who are morally or intellectually so color-blind that they cannot distinguish anything but pure white and pure black, and because pure whiteness and pure blackness are not to be found either in individuals or nations, they avoid aligning themselves with goodness because it is not perfection. War saved Greek civilization from the Persians; it secured American independence; it freed the slaves and preserved the Union.

I regard it as eminently proper to use science to prevent crime and to apprehend and punish criminals, whether they be common thieves or international brigands. When we confront an aggressor who has no scruples against using all possible means to gain his violent ends, there is no rule of sportsmanship to deter us from beating him at his own game. If he attacks us with machine guns, it is folly to limit our defense to popguns.

The Meaning of the War

We should have prevented the present criminal rampage by peaceful means. I was not one of those who regarded the task we assumed in 1917 as finished with the signing of the Armistice in November, 1918. I added my feeble voice during the ensuing year to the plea for collective security, a security we should now dearly love to have. We fought to "make the world safe for democracy," but we got tired and did not finish the job; instead, we buried our heads in the sands of isolation. It was not that we fought for an illusion, but that we allowed nearsighted men to throw away the fruits of a victory which we, not they, had won. The conclusion should be, not that it is futile to defend democracy, but that we must do it over again, as often as necessary, to make the world safe at least for *our* democracy, and that we must turn a deaf ear to those who can see no better way to keep out the plague than to bar the windows and doors. I am not one who fears that a democracy commits suicide by going to war. More democracies have emerged from war than have succumbed to it. I think President Hutchins is wrong in his history. The worst dictatorships have arisen in times not of war, but of depression.

Those who accuse science of responsibility for the destructiveness of warfare overlook the power of science also to reconstruct. The destruction may not be an unmixed evil. We may hope for a new city to arise on the site of the slums of London. The destruction of life is a more serious matter. Nevertheless, let us not be maudlin over the loss of life through bombs while we remain complacent about the far larger loss of life through automobiles, preventable disease, and unhealthful living conditions.

I have enough faith in the essential nobility of the human race to hope that the view of life as something to be prolonged at whatever cost of ideals is a mere passing phase of cynical individualism. I rejoice in the example set by the Finns, the Greeks, the British, and now the Serbs; men who are willing to risk their lives against fearful odds in the conviction that it is better to die like men on their feet than to live somewhat longer on their knees.

I trust that this statement of my position will prevent the following discussion of concrete relations of science to war from appearing too cold-blooded. It is the product not only of scientific and military experience, but of deep convictions as well.

War, discipline, and scientific method.—If a people are determined to survive, not merely as individuals but also economically and culturally, they must be alert to the various elements contributing to national strength. Any exhaustive analysis of these factors would take us far beyond the limits of this address. If I neglect many of them, it is not through failure to appreciate their importance, but in order to emphasize science as one factor which is indispensable. Moreover, the science I wish to present for the purpose is not merely the "classified knowledge" as defined by the dictionary and preserved in scientific books and in the heads of scientific authorities; it is more particularly that combination of knowledge, attitudes, and skills known as "scientific method." The scientific man is not so much a person who knows a great deal about his field as he is one who can tackle new problems therein with good prospects for success.

The power of the scientific habit of mind to contribute to national defense is illustrated by a long succession of ideas and inventions to be found in military history. As I present a few selected examples, I should like you to bear in mind that military training is commonly thought of in terms of discipline and obedience. While respect for authority is an essential factor in military efficiency, the trouble comes from the fact that the authority is based so largely upon experience with the past. The future, however, is not likely to reproduce the past at all accurately; hence a somewhat different outlook is required in order to deal with it successfully—an elasticity of mind that all too few possess. It is hard to appreciate the fact that while the next war will be similar to the last, it will also be different. Even though the innovations constitute but a small proportion of the total, they are likely to be most disturbing. If a game of chess were to be altered by changing the kind of move for only one of the pieces, it would seriously revolutionize the entire game. My contention is that the war game cannot be counted upon to remain the mere maneuvering of troops on the field of battle, like the pieces in a standard game of chess. Your opponent will, if he can, introduce new pieces that move in unorthodox ways. To appreciate this, all you would have to do would be to substitute for one of your bishops a piece which you could call a "tank" and which could take two opposing pieces at a time instead of one. A book on chess would give you no advice on how to meet the situation; you would have to figure it out for yourself.

Now let us turn to a few samples of innovations such as an enemy with an elastic type of mind may be expected to intro-

Hildebrand: Science 43

duce. I like to cite in this connection Gideon's attack upon the Midianites, as described in the Old Testament. Gideon first of all pared down his army to a rather small body of men who were not afraid of a fight. He equipped them, in addition to their regular arms, with trumpets and torches hidden within earthenware pitchers. They sneaked up on the Midianite camp at night, then, on a given signal, uncovered their torches, threw their pitchers to the earth with a big crash, blew a great blast on their trumpets and shouted, and annihilated the panic-stricken Midianites. Gideon had the type of mind which could utilize mechanical devices as well as psychology.

Consider next the Greek phalanx. This was a compact mass of men bristling with spears like a huge porcupine. It became the basic element of Greek military tactics. Eventually, however, the Romans devised a method for coping with the unwieldy phalanx. They equipped their legionaries with short swords with which they could dive under the protruding spears and cut up the Greek warriors at close range. That sealed the doom of the phalanx.

Again, you may remember that during the Punic Wars the Romans thought of a device to neutralize the superior naval skill of the Carthaginians. They equipped their galleys with huge drawbridges armed with spikes at the far end, which, when lowered to the deck of an enemy ship, would bind the two ships together and allow the Romans to swarm over on the Carthaginian ships and take advantage of their superior skill in close combat.

The longbow of the English, pitted against the heavily

armored chivalry of France at Agincourt, resulted in 5000 French dead and 1000 prisoners, with a loss of but 113 English. You may read in the *Encyclopedia Britannica* that "the moral lesson of the battle was the incapacity of a military caste to learn from experience and to adapt their traditions intelligently to new needs." The *Monitor* revolutionized naval construction. The German submarine in the last World War almost nullified English sea power. British tanks, which broke through at Cambrai, might have won the war then for the Allies had they been used on a larger scale. The first German gas attack left a swath to the English Channel entirely undefended and, had it been executed with more confidence, might have won the war for Germany at that time. The mustard-gas-filled artillery shell, fired on the British by the Germans some time later, appeared at first to be a joke, on account of the delayed effects of this terrific substance, but it turned out to be anything but a joke. When I arrived in France in January, 1918, we were flooded with problems connected with this new weapon. The gas mask protected the eyes and respiratory tract, but how to protect the skin, how to get mustard gas out of infected clothing, how to remove it from material on which it had splashed, how to neutralize it in shellholes, what fabrics would be resistant to its passage—these were all problems pressing for solution.

The varieties of gas offered tactical possibilities as diverse as those afforded by other weapons. Lacrimators and sternutators produced their characteristic violent effects in extremely small concentrations. A single lacrimator shell dropped on a crossroads along which trucks must pass might put many drivers temporarily out of action. An unexpected bit of it in the eyes of artillerymen might silence a battery. The effects of several other gases were delayed rather than immediate. Some gases disappeared as fast as the wind blew them away. Other and less volatile substances disappeared only slowly, the rate depending upon weather conditions. We went so far as to devise "fake" gases. We prepared a compound which smelled more like mustard gas than mustard gas itself, if one could judge from the testimony of the Chemical Warfare Service officers on our post. Such a substance could be used in the following way. It was understood on both sides that any terrain which had been shelled with mustard gas would not be used as an avenue of attack and hence need not be heavily defended. Suppose, now, that our side should shell a certain region with the fake mustard gas. The enemy would feel a sense of security, thinking it to be the true mustard gas, and could leave that region comparatively undefended. Our side, knowing it to be harmless, could then attack at that point, reaping a great advantage.

One of the most remarkable examples of a novel technique was demonstrated by the Finns in their recent struggle against the numerically superior Russian army. The skill and intelligence shown by the operations of their ski troops constitute a bright page in the annals of heroic military history.

The airplane introduced novel elements into the last World War, chiefly in the realm of reconnoitering and artillery fire control. The plane became the eyes of the army. The French army of several years ago was advertised as the best in the world, but its high command was evidently living in the past, expecting to win the next war as it had won the last. The Germans did not suffer from the complacency that so easily follows success, and turned to new methods for winning the present war, with the result that the airplane is now filling entirely new functions. These functions themselves represent a continual battle between scientific and technical resources, as well as the skill of the pilots. Anyone following the news closely can see evidences of this in the continually shifting methods employed.

Some of the foregoing illustrations represent crude applications of science, others are rather complex. The longbow is a simple device. The modern airplane is a complicated machine, the produce of the brains of thousands of engineers and workmen. Both of them represent, however, essentially the same combination of alertness and intelligent command of the means available. They represent the very antithesis of reliance upon a Delphic oracle or upon traditional instruction or mere confidence in numerical strength. They typify qualities which make a nation strong in time of peace, as well as in time of war.

Scientific insight and national defense.—Now resistance to new ideas is enormous, and to overcome it is a major problem for a nation attempting to defend itself. During the first World War, both sides had certain rules regarding gas attacks. One of these was that a gas attack should be attempted only when the wind was blowing toward the enemy at the rate of from 4 to 7 miles per hour. If the velocity of the wind were greater, the gas would blow away too soon; if it were less, the direction of the wind was precarious and the cloud might turn around and drift back upon the attacking force. In accordance with this distinction, the Germans had signs, "GASWIND," which were posted at times when the wind was such as to make a gas attack upon them a possibility. It was very important *then* to have their gas masks at hand. When the signs were not posted, corresponding care did not need to be taken. An intelligent British colonel, commander of gas troops, knew about this rule and the German faith therein. He therefore decided upon a most unusual and unorthodox course. He carried out a gas attack with Livens projectors when the wind was blowing at the rate of 11 miles per hour toward the British lines. His own men were prepared and wore their gas masks, whereas the enemy was taken completely by surprise and suffered an enormous number of casualties. The report made by the German commander to his superior regarding this operation was captured, and the British were amused to read therein a bitter complaint against the violation of the rules by the British commander.

An order was issued in the American army to the effect that attacking troops should follow their barrage as closely as possible, even at the risk of "shorts," in order to take advantage of the enemy while he was most disorganized. At the same time, there was another rule to the effect that troops should not be ordered to advance following a gas attack until after a long time had elapsed. This difference was evidently due to the fact that the officers who made the rules were less familiar with gas and therefore much more afraid of it than they were of shrapnel. It seemed to us, however, that the principle which had led to the former rule should also be applied to the latter case. We knew that our new idea would have little chance of acceptance unless put, as it were, in words of one syllable. We therefore had a motion picture taken of a gas cloud traveling down our experimental field, while showing in the same frame a squad of soldiers without gas masks walking right behind the cloud. We had another picture taken of the same men the next day, to show that they were still hale and hearty.

The French used an artillery gas shell filled in part with hydrogen cyanide. They had shown the effectiveness of this gas by experiments on dogs. While attending a French gas school, I was present at a demonstration of its efficacy. Some Paris street dogs had been tied up in trenches, and a few bombs containing hydrogen cyanide were exploded a short distance to windward. By the time we reached the trench, within a half-minute after the attack, the dogs were as dead as doornails. Indeed, we used this substance at the Experimental Field of the Chemical Warfare Service to kill dogs for purposes of autopsy. If one or two drops of the liquid were placed upon the tongue of a dog, he would be entirely still within fifteen or twenty seconds. At the British experimental field, however, experiments had been performed using different animals with the same gas, and the conclusion was reached that one could not rely upon the results on any one animal in order to infer the toxicity for man. It turned out that dogs proved to be hypersensitive to hydrogen cyanide. Professor Barcroft, a noted British physiologist, undertook to demonstrate this fact in a way that would be unmistakable to the authorities responsible for providing poison-gas shells.

Hildebrand: Science

He took a live dog with him into a gas chamber, turned on the hydrogen cyanide, stayed until the dog was dead, and then came out. Having myself experienced the involuntary effects upon one's nervous system of going into a gas chamber under similar circumstances, even though all had been arranged so as to involve no possible danger but only discomfort, I can assure you that this was an act of extraordinary heroism.

In the last World War an officer was standing beside an American general, who pointed to a distant wood, saying: "Look at the enemy advancing into that wood. I shelled that place with gas about eight hours ago." The other asked: "What kind of gas?" The general replied: "What gas? Oh, just gas." Now a modicum of scientific insight would have revealed to a man properly trained the absurdity of confusing a true gas, such as phosgene, which would drift away in the wind, with a so-called gas such as mustard, which is scarcely more volatile than sewing-machine oil and might remain for days. Ah, but you say, "You can't expect a field officer to be a scientist!" This general, however, had been a professor of military science and tactics; surely, he should have been able to appreciate a few kindergarten facts about the materials he was using.

Again, a British chemist suggested the use of mustard gas as early as 1915, but the army authority to whom the idea was presented could not see its possibilities until, two years later, the Germans used it against the British with terrible effect. Illustrations of this sort could be multiplied at length.

This slowness on the part of many military and naval men

to invent or even appreciate novel ideas has been deplored by members of both services. Admiral Sims once stated: "That military men are conservative admits of no doubt. Whether they are more so than civilians is beside the question. The important point is that their conservatism may be so dangerous that it is highly important that they should so train their minds in logical thinking as to eliminate, or at least minimize, this danger." Again, in a minority report as a member of the Board of Visitors of the United States Naval Academy, he said: "It is an outstanding fact that the Navy has never initiated any one of the really fundamental reforms that were essential to bring it to its present efficiency. All of these reforms were forced upon the Navy from the outside and in every case against determined opposition, and the Navy still resists perfectly legitimate criticism."

My purpose in giving the foregoing examples is not to attack the Army or the Navy; indeed, the attitudes about which I am complaining are prevalent in all human activities. Only a minority of people have the imagination and initiative to introduce changes, or have the judgment necessary to advocate sound innovations. The majority always take refuge in tradition, in formulas, in prejudice, in emotional hostility to novel ideas. The scientific habit of mind alone can overcome these obstacles.

Incidentally, you young men who go into training camps will make a grievous mistake if you look forward dully to being mere pawns in the game. As a former commandant of a military post, I can assure you that there, as everywhere, those with initiative, skills, and brains can find opportunities to use them.

That the barriers of inertia must be continually overcome should be ever more evident from the changing character of warfare. War is continually becoming less and less the mere maneuvering of troops on the battlefield and more and more the exploitation of the full scientific and engineering resources of the nation. There are many who still picture our possible role in the present war in terms of our part in the last. They still think of masses of men holding trenches. It would be sensible for them to get up to date. The recent operations in Belgium and France were carried out by smaller concentrations of men in machines. The defense of England today depends on men operating machinery: airplanes, ships, tanks, and artillery. These weapons, moreover, are undergoing constant alterations. Several years ago we heard of Italian air power in terms of numbers of planes. The events of recent months have, however, shown these planes to be obsolete and at the mercy of the newer, improved planes of the Royal Air Force. One who has followed closely even the meager information in the public press can hardlly have failed to get some inkling of the extent to which aerial warfare has been a continual contest not only of flying skill, but also of engineering and physics applied with almost feverish intensity.

The cultivation of scientific aptitude.—One lesson we should draw from all this is that scientific aptitude is so important as to deserve the fullest development and scope. It must begin in school. Physical science must be taught by teachers equipped for their task by enthusiasm for science, by native intelligence, and by sound training. These qualities cannot be guaranteed by certificates based on units in pedagogy and school administration or stimulated by a philosophy of education which encourages a child to think that the universe revolves about him as its center. The teaching of science must emphasize experiment, observation, and analysis rather than soaking up facts and definitions from textbooks. Its success should be estimated honestly in terms of understanding phyisco-chemical phenomena rather than more remote aims such as "citizenship" and "the worthy use of leisure." Those who are unable to travel very far along this uphill path should be set at tasks within their powers and not retard others capable of climbing toward the goal. In every high school there are many boys, if not girls, who can fairly eat up the fascinating, concrete, and practical material presented in these fields. The nation's essential supply of scientists and engineers can be kept up only if the schools do their duty in this matter.

The proper foundation must also include a sound and adequate mathematical training. Mathematics is a language far superior to English for dealing with many important ideas and relationships. It must be practiced to the point of facility by those who will be concerned with such matters. There has been a dangerous move on the part of some school administrators to deny students the opportunity to develop adequate mathematical facility. Mathematics, like foreign languages, is crowded to the point of inefficiency by subjects such as "social living," "personal management," and "core curriculum." The solid disciplines for which I plead need not monopolize the curriculum, but it is the height of folly to emasculate them in favor of classes designed to develop personal glamour or the mere emotions of patriotism without the capacity to serve their country effectively. I judge from the numerous screen magazines based upon Hollywood that the country's supply of glamour is more than adequate and that other objectives might well claim more attention from citizens even in this great city and county which has cornered the world's supply of egocentric talent. A good formula for success is to enter a field that is not overcrowded.

I would carry my message to the next stage by pleading that colleges and universities do more than they do at present to develop scientific habits of mind among students of science. We should not talk glibly about scientific method and then write examinations calling for little more than memory. We should not wince when an uninformed public accuses us of being poor teachers because we are too busy with research; we should rather make it evident that only that teacher of science who has enough curiosity to ask nature some hitherto unanswered questions can hope to arouse a similar curiosity among his students. We can, if we will, try to be not "schoolmarms" and martinets but leaders of exciting explorations, treating our students as apprentices rather than slaves. And regardless of whether the present threat to our free way of life is of short or long duration—and it may be long, thanks to our procrastination—our supply of trained intelligence must be maintained and our universities kept functioning efficiently.

I wish I had it in my power to apply my theory to West Point and Annapolis by changing them into graduate professional schools, recruited from graduates of our colleges.

These two academies are too far removed from the scientific spirit. Their instructors do no research and the cadets have little stimulus of the sort present in a good department of physics or an active engineering school.

Next, I would provide for a much closer contact of scientific men with the Army and Navy. This was woefully lacking at the outbreak of the World War and took months to establish. It is far better now, but it can never be too close. Even now there is too much reliance upon officers to discover the problems. It takes an inventor to see what to invent; it takes a physicist to see the possibilities of physics. Such men should, therefore, be made intimately acquainted at firsthand with military operations. When they work at long range they neither get the significant problems nor devise practical solutions.

Science and democratic society.—Finally, I should like to express my conviction that science and democratic society are complementary. German efficiency up to the present is living on the legacy of an earlier period during which that nation, though only partly democratic in government, nevertheless gave the world the academic and democratic ideal of freedom to teach and to learn. Today the sources of scientific knowledge in Germany have been partly dried up. A large proportion of its best scientific men have either fled or been dismissed and often persecuted. I am not speaking in ignorance. I have lived in Germany under Kaiser, Republic, and Hitler. The springs of fundamental science which feed applied science, technology, industry, and national defense are now flowing more freely in England than in Germany, and more freely still in America. They will serve us in peace as they now provide the sinews of war. The scientific men and the students of science are not the ones who are today hanging back as the nation calls them to serve; they have seen the persecution of their German confreres. Would that those responsible for our present labor disputes were similarly farsighted enough to learn from the fate of their confreres in France the folly of domestic strife in the presence of a foreign enemy.

Those who complain that our country is not good enough to be worth defending are not the scientists. They are not the ones who insist on talking when they should be working. Their conception of democracy is not Kipling's Bandar Log, the monkeys who chattered like some United States senators about what great people they were, but who never united to get anything done.

But now, in conclusion, although I have been stressing the role of science in building national strength, let me again assure you that I do not regard science as sufficient. Equally necessary are certain moral qualities: vision, purpose, courage. The achievements of mankind have been wrought by men who have seen difficulties not as barriers but as challenges; who have preferred adventure to security; labor to luxury; men who have accepted the world as it is and made the best of it; who have not whined because their ancestors have not made it more to their liking.

Speaking as one of them, I would paint good old Uncle Sam not as senile, feeble, and fearful, hiding under the bedclothes, trembling lest he attract the attention of the burglar rifling his pockets, but rather as still the hardy pioneer he once was; who won his freedom by fighting for it; who fought again to make men free; who scorns now the counsel of fear and the temptations of luxury; who is bold and wise enough when threatened by a tough to show himself ready to be equally tough.

THE IMPACT OF THE WAR ON THE ECONOMIC RELATIONS OF THE UNITED STATES AND LATIN AMERICA

GORDON S. WATKINS
PROFESSOR OF ECONOMICS
IN THE UNIVERSITY OF CALIFORNIA

Lecture delivered April 15, 1941

THE IMPACT OF THE WAR ON THE ECONOMIC RELATIONS OF THE UNITED STATES AND LATIN AMERICA

WHATEVER may be the ultimate effects of the present war in Europe, one of the most significant immediate effects of the conflict is the rediscovery of Latin America by North Americans. Thanks to Germany's irrepressible *Weltanschauung* and her persistent drive for world domination, Pan-American security has become almost an obsession in the minds of our statesmen who are deeply concerned about the political and economic repercussions of a possible German triumph. Latin America, once only a vaguely definable geographical area to most North Americans, suddenly has become a region of paramount importance in the total defense of the Western Hemisphere. Political and economic coöperation among all the Americas is now an integral part of our national policy; cold indifference is yielding to the warmth of genuine friendship and good neighborliness.

Those in high places who are responsible for the formulation of our national and international policy recognize clearly that friendship and trust are fundamental to both military and economic coöperation. Until recent years distrust and suspicion rather than confidence and good will were characteristic of international relations among the Americas. Even in recent weeks the behavior of the United States Senate in its deliberations concerning the purchase of Argentine beef by this nation's military forces certainly has done nothing to dispel the fear and suspicion which our Latin American neighbors traditionally have manifested toward us. But the outlook for our Good Neighbor policy is certainly much brighter now.

Land and population.—An analysis of the impact of the second World War upon the economic relations of the Americas is impossible without a glance at the vast area and population involved. Altogether there are approximately 275,000,000 people living in the Americas. Of this number, three-fifths are in North America, about one-third in South America, and only about 8 per cent in Central America and the West Indian islands. About 90 per cent of the entire population of the Americas live in ten of the twenty-two countries, and almost one-half of the total is in the United States.[1]

North America, including the United States, Canada, and Mexico, has a land area of eight million square miles. *South America,* including Brazil, Argentina, Bolivia, Peru, Colombia, Venezuela, Ecuador, Paraguay, Uruguay, Chile, and British, Dutch, and French Guiana, has a land area of more than seven million square miles. *Central America and the Caribbean region,* including Nicaragua, Honduras, Cuba, Guatemala, Panama, Costa Rica, the Dominican Republic, El Salvador, Haiti, Puerto Rico, the British West Indies, and other foreign possessions, have a land area of 371,000 square miles.[2] The two continents and numerous islands which constitute the Americas have a total area of 15,500,000 square miles. In any man's language that is a lot of square mileage;

---

[1] U.S. Bureau of Foreign and Domestic Commerce (Department of Commerce), *Foreign Commerce Yearbook,* 1938, p. 386.

[2] *Ibid.*

it suggests the practical difficulties which confront those who seek to build unity and coöperation. The total distribution of land among the three Americas is 52 per cent for North America, 46 per cent for South America, and only 2 per cent for Central America and the West Indies.[3]

The three Americas differ widely in the distribution of people. For the most part North America is characterized by thickly settled industrial areas, many large industrial centers, large fertile agricultural regions fairly thickly settled, and by wide areas of thinly populated range, forests, and desert wastes. South America, on the contrary, is characterized by industrial areas highly concentrated in a few very large centers, usually close by the ocean or at some major port, with the remaining population thinly distributed over large areas of tropical forests, mountains, or plains. In Central America and the Caribbean islands there are densely populated agricultural regions in the tropical lowlands, and much more thinly populated highlands and plateaus behind the coasts. Throughout the Americas, interesting racial mixtures create a serious problem for those who dream of the unity of the Western Hemisphere.

Economic resources.—If, as is currently suspected, Adolph Hitler casts a covetous eye at the Americas as potential colonies of the Greater Germany, his behavior is quite understandable. Here are green pastures, productive plantations, rich ranchos, and vast supplies of precious minerals.[4] It is not

---
[3] *Ibid.*
[4] See Mordecai Ezekiel, "Economic Relations between the Americas," *International Conciliation,* Carnegie Endowment for International Peace, Division of Intercourse and Education, No. 367, February, 1941.

62 *The Meaning of the War*

strange that he has nostalgically sighed: "What could not Germany do with such lands as these!" Economic motivation plays a significant role in Hitler's behavior; it provides wings for the extraordinary flights of his fertile imagination. And well it might, for here are vast treasures that have always lured the covetous buccaneer and challenged the daring spirits of the explorers.

South American lands have produced a great part of the world's wheat and coffee, pastured a considerable proportion of the world's livestock, and yielded up great stores of minerals and oil to supply the needs of mankind. Copper and nitrates have been contributed by Chile, tin and other minerals by Bolivia, and petroleum by Venezuela. In each of these countries mineral resources have been developed largely by foreign capital, and a high percentage of the value of exports has gone to the support of investors in other lands. In Mexico, the production, refining, and export of gold and silver, petroleum and its products, lead, zinc, copper, and other minerals are major industries, while her iron and steel manufacture now meets three-fourths of her domestic needs. In Colombia, gold and platinum are important, although less so than coffee. Brazil has the world's richest undeveloped deposits of high-grade iron ore, and coal, manganese, gold, and silver in large amounts. Compared with those of the United States, the mineral resources of Central and South America are scarcely touched. Countries south of the Rio Grande now produce two-fifths of the world's silver, nearly one-fourth of its copper and its tin, and one-seventh of its petroleum.[5]

---
[5] *Ibid.*, p. 100.

Nor is the picture less rosy when one surveys agricultural resources. Argentina is properly characterized as the greatest agricultural nation of South America, and one of its most important industrial nations. Her land produces three-fourths of the world's trade in meat, and two-thirds of the world's linseed; she is the world's greatest exporter of corn, and its second largest exporter of wheat and wool. Today fully 97 per cent of her exports are agricultural and pastoral products.

Brazil, a quarter of a million square miles larger than the United States, provides another example of Latin American richness in agricultural resources. Brazil's fertile soil yields almost every crop known to man. Coffee, corn, beans, wheat, tea, rice, sugar, cotton, and all kinds of fruit are among the numerous products easily grown. As yet only 3 per cent of her arable land is under cultivation. There are other products covetously eyed by nations in search of raw materials, such as rubber, hard woods, tropical nuts, and natural dyes. Brazil's rubber trade disappeared when the British and the Dutch planted rubber trees in the East Indies, where crude rubber has been produced so scientifically and so cheaply that that region now supplies 90 per cent of the world's trade.

Similar details could be furnished concerning the rich mineral and agricultural resources of the other Latin American countries, but enough has been said to indicate why these countries constitute a powerful magnet for nations in search of foodstuffs, raw materials, outlets for surplus population, and markets for finished goods.

The effects of the war.—Sustained exportation of agricultural and mineral products is an indispensable condition of

Latin America's economic welfare and progress. Whenever foreign markets for the normal export trade disappear, distress is immediate and severe. This fact has been quite generally recognized as the Achilles heel in the economic defense of the Western Hemisphere. The United States export trade takes less than 10 per cent of her total annual production, while Latin American countries export from one-third to one-half of their commodity output. In some countries the ratio rises as high as 70 to 80 per cent. In Chile, Colombia, and Venezuela about nine-tenths or more of all mineral production is exported, and in Peru about three-fourths. Most agricultural exporting countries, such as Brazil and Colombia, export about one-half of their farm ouput. The Argentine exports two-thirds of its crops and three-fourths of its livestock, and Cuba, with its intensive sugar production, exports more than three-fourths of her farm produce.[6]

The initial effect of the outbreak of the second World War in September, 1939, was to cause a sharp speculative rise in the prices of the principal export crops from the Western Hemisphere. Prices of sugar, cotton, corn, cacao beans, wool, hides and skins, meats, tin, and copper advanced sharply, but a discouraging price reaction came within succeeding months. Coffee, the principal export crop of Brazil and Colombia, as well as of several smaller countries, did not experience even the brief stimulus of demand which characterized the markets for other products.

The almost immediate decline in foreign markets that followed the outbreak of war was nowhere more severely felt

---

[6] Ezekiel, *ibid.*, p. 108.

than in Latin America, whose trade with Europe in normal times is so important. The German-controlled market was closed almost immediately. The extension of the war area in the spring of 1940, the collapse of France, and the entrance of Italy into the conflict resulted in the almost complete disappearance of European outlets for the export surpluses of Latin America. "For the twenty American republics in the South this meant that new buyers had to be found for about $500,000,000 worth of raw materials, or 28 to 29 per cent of the total yearly exports, the amount customarily going to the European markets now closed."[7] Similarly, imports from Germany and other Central European countries were sharply reduced or stopped completely, affecting import trade.

Under the prevailing circumstances the United States afforded the most natural and convenient source of imports for Latin America. "Exports from the United States to this region increased in value about 42 per cent when compared with exports of the twelve months preceding the outbreak of the war."[8] Serious hardships were soon experienced by the importing nations because of the necessity of buying goods at the prevailing higher price levels obtaining in the United States and paying higher freight rates. The disappearance of European markets as a result of the war had seriously reduced the purchasing power of the food and raw-material exporting countries of Latin America. British import control further diminished the outlets for surplus products. Dollar exchange was not adequate to underwrite an expansion of imports from the United States.

[7] *Ibid.*, p. 126.   [8] *Ibid.*

The United States increased the value of its imports from Latin America to the extent of 31 per cent during the first year of the war compared with the preceding year, but this was not sufficient to compensate for the loss of European markets. Heavy shipments of gold and silver, the inflow of refugee funds, and loans from the United States Export-Import Bank helped to maintain purchases in this country. The cold fact is that were it not for the extension of loans to Latin America by the Export-Import Bank the internal buying power of our southern neighbors would be much more seriously affected. But such loans cover only a portion of the losses resulting from the collapse of the European market.

Difficulties confronting the United States in improving trade relations with Latin America.—The earnest efforts of the United States government to assist Latin American countries out of their distressing dilemma and to implement the Good Neighbor policy that is so essential to an enlightened Pan-Americanism have met with discouraging rebuffs. This situation is understandable in the light of certain historical facts. Politically, there has been no natural or essential bond of unity among the Americas. This is due to the fact that the democratic liberalism manifested in the representative government of the United States has had no counterpart in the feudalistic and undemocratic dictatorships of South America. Whether we like it or not, it is true that the political theory and practice of our southern neighbors have had much more in common with the totalitarian pattern than with the democratic ideas and processes of the United States.

A more serious obstacle to genuine Pan-Americanism has

been the persistent fear and suspicion manifested by many Latin American countries toward the United States. Whenever the United States, the wealthiest, most powerful, and most advanced nation in the New World, has, without invitation, assumed the guardianship of the Western Hemisphere, suspicion rather than gratitude has been the immediate reaction from our neighbors. The unpleasant fact is that the United States has often been regarded with greater distrust than any European or Asiatic nation. This is perhaps partly a matter of geographic proximity, but it is partly the natural result of our unwise foreign policy. Unfortunately, the "Colossus of the North," as Latin Americans often call this country, appears to many Latin American minds as a menace much more real and dangerous than the widely publicized peril of foreign ideologies. One writer has observed: "Domination by a European power seems far less to be feared than the actual fact of domination by American financial interests, backed by a State Department devoted to the principles of 'Dollar Diplomacy.' "[9] The Monroe Doctrine has been a veritable red rag to Latin America; our neighbors have often interpreted that doctrine as an instrument designed to keep foreign powers out of this hemisphere in order that the United States might have freedom of action.

Whatever may be the reasons for this attitude of distrust and fear, and they have been many and real, no such indictment is applicable to the Good Neighbor policy of this nation in recent years. But the change in our foreign policy has not prevented the Fascist and National Socialist powers (Ger-

---

[9] Katherine Carr, *South American Primer*, p. 152.

many, Italy, and Spain) from fanning into a flame the dying embers of traditional suspicion. These European haters of American democracy have not hesitated to try to persuade our Latin American neighbors that our present program of hemisphere protection is but a smokescreen for imperialistic expansion. In this regard the language of the Fascists and National Socialists has a brotherly resemblance to that of the Communists, whose dislike of American institutions is no less wholehearted. Unless this propaganda of fear and suspicion can be diminished, if not obliterated, effective economic cooperation and hemisphere defense are going to be difficult to achieve. The second World War has considerably altered our point of view with regard to Latin America. The loss of our foreign trade, except that with the British Empire, has made us conscious of the potential importance of Latin American markets. The belligerency of increasingly powerful totalitarian states has made unmistakably clear the need for adequate defense if the democratic ideal is to survive in this hemisphere.

The Fascist–National Socialist peril.—The new political and economic policy and program of the United States for the Western Hemisphere are constructed on the assumption that penetration of Fascism and National Socialism into Latin America constitutes a menace to the political security and economic progress of the constituent republics. How real is this menace, and what is its medium of expression? From certain vantage points the peril appears very real, from others it seems relatively insignificant. A brief examination of the problem will reveal both of these aspects.

On the one side is the significant fact that even prior to the outbreak of the present war the United States was selling more goods to Latin America than Germany, Italy, Japan, and Great Britain combined, despite the German trade and propaganda drive and the heavy investments of British capital in that area. Moreover, our share of Latin American trade has constantly increased, even when the Axis trade was proclaimed to be making spectacular progress. Germany's trade gains prior to the outbreak of hostilities were largely at the expense of Great Britain, and were the direct consequence of the German system of controlled foreign exchange trading and barter arrangements. The most striking fact about Latin American trade is not the growth of Axis trade, but rather that the United States has continued to dominate a market in which she buys relatively so little.

The fact that we buy so little in a market in which we sell so much is the vulnerable spot in our Latin American trade relations and constitutes the index to the other aspect of our problem. The United States does not want Argentine meat or wheat, or Brazilian cotton, and therefore our trading position is basically weak in comparison with that of the Axis. Conversely, here the Axis position is strong. Germany wants foodstuffs and raw materials; she is eager to buy the products which Latin America, in order to survive, must sell. Japan needs Brazil's cotton and is eager to sell and buy in Latin American markets. Italy, like Germany, needs the foodstuffs and raw materials of the Americas and desires an increase in her volume of trade with them.

German production, it must be remembered, is controlled

production, and whenever possible world prices are purposely kept at conveniently low levels. Through the medium of barter and direct exchange Germany offers her Latin American customers more for their products than world markets will give. Through Askimarks, or compensation marks, and clearing agreements Germany obtains the raw materials she needs in exchange for machinery, machine tools, and other manufactured goods which Latin America wants. The Askimark differs from the ordinary blocked currency, which is available for certain purposes to anyone, in that this type of mark is available only to the exporter to whom it is issued for the purchase of specific commodities in Germany. This means that Germany may buy up exportable surpluses at prices quite above the level prevailing in other markets, make payment in Askimarks, and then charge what price she wishes for the commodities for which these marks are exchanged. Nor has Germany hesitated to substitute other goods for those originally specified for purchase with Askimarks, when she was unable to make proper deliveries. Consequently, many of her customers have found themselves with goods that they could not conveniently use—like the Standard Oil Company, which was compelled to accept a consignment of harmonicas and Christmas toys in exchange for oil, or leave the balance blocked in Germany.[10]

In order to obtain important advantages in trade with South and Central American countries, Germany has vigorously bought up surplus products which she did not immediately

---

[10] For a discussion of this subject see Clark Foreman and Joan Raushenbush, *Total Defense* (New York: Doubleday, Doran & Co., 1940).

need, making payment in Askimarks, then disposing of these surpluses in direct competition with the same countries, lowering the price so as to undersell the original producer. This has been done with respect to coffee from Colombia, beans from Chile, and numerous products from Argentina and Brazil.[11] Once she has established herself as the sole or principal market for a specific product, Germany then threatens to discontinue her purchases completely unless desired economic and political concessions are made as a basis for further trade. In a period when other markets have been restricted, the high prices offered by Germany have proved attractive to exporters who have high-pressured their governments into continuing trade agreements with her. Moreover, the accumulation of blocked balances in Germany arising from previous sales of goods to her means that many nations are compelled to continue trading with her long after they have discovered the disadvantages of such trade and wish to be free from its restrictions.[12]

There comes a time when rational nations no longer desire to barter nitrates or cotton or meat or coffee for luxuries, armaments, toys, and harmonicas. Moreover, because of the British blockade, German deliveries have not only been delayed for periods of several months but now have practically ceased. Even such goods as have been delivered have been of inferior quality, poorly or hastily made for the export trade, and often of an obsolete model or style. There is reason to believe that, unless Germany wins the war, her barter system has reached its peak, as far as Latin America is concerned.

---

[11] Ezekiel, *op. cit.*, p. 124.   [12] *Ibid.*

Its inflexibility is an inherent weakness that will cause it to decline or disappear if and when freer markets are restored in other countries.

Perhaps more greatly to be feared than the overestimated economic penetration of Latin America by the Axis powers is the political penetration to which the trade relations of such powers are often the prelude. Through the lanes of commerce have traveled waves of Fascist and Nazi propaganda, indoctrination of Axis ideology, and subtle suggestions for organizing and administering political institutions. It is generally admitted that German and Italian propaganda is incessant, persuasive, and skillfully managed.

German and Italian colonies in South America are at once the bases and the targets for the mass output of the propaganda ministries. Not only do the substantial minorities of Germans and Italians in South America naturally prefer direct trade with the totalitarian countries, but they are the logical nerve centers for the dissemination of Axis political ideology. Brazil has some 900,000 Germans and 2,000,000 Italians; Argentina has 236,000 Germans and 3,000,000 Italians; Uruguay's population of 2,093,331 is one-third Italian and there are 10,000 Germans. By transatlantic radio and through the foreign-language press a constant stream of propaganda dealing with racial superiority, antisemitism, the inevitable triumph of Fascism and National Socialism, and the equally inevitable fall of the "inefficient democracies," flows to Latin America.

What can the United States do about it?—The extent to which the menace of Fascism and National Socialism in Latin

America can be combated effectively depends very largely upon the wisdom and generosity of the political and economic policy which the United States will apply in her relations with her neighbors. Politically, we must recognize the extreme sensitivity of Latin Americans. In a very real sense we are now much more dependent upon the good will of Latin American countries than they are upon our good will toward them. The United States has much more to lose from European aggression in Central and South America than have the Latin Americans themselves. This is because democratic institutions have as yet obtained only a feeble footing in the southern countries, and the numerous dictatorships already established in them represent only an insignificant percentage of the people. Whether they share in the government of their countries or not, Latin Americans resent foreign aggression, regardless of its source.

If the United States is to gain the confidence and coöperation of its neighbors it may have to redefine the Monroe Doctrine with a view to giving positive assurance of noninterference in the internal political affairs of Latin America's sovereign states. In return for such a guaranty of independent sovereignty and self-determination, the United States may properly ask for a reciprocal guaranty of Latin American coöperation in the defense of the Western Hemisphere, not only against invasion by hostile foreign powers, but also against the equally destructive invasion of foreign ideologies. International boundaries constitute no barrier to the migration of ideas, but intelligent vigilance can preclude the dissemination of undesirable economic-political philosophies.

The Meaning of the War

The success of political coöperation will depend very largely upon the effectiveness of economic coöperation. No amount of well-meaning expression of good will and good neighborliness will accomplish much unless it is translated into terms of economic action. The economic plight of the Latin American countries is a serious one, and in the postwar period it may be more serious still.

The future of inter-American trade will undoubtedly depend upon the outcome of the present war. If the democratic countries should win, comparative freedom of trade may again prevail; nations may again develop economic security and prosperity through the exchange of raw materials for the essentials and luxuries of life. Much will depend upon the intelligence of the treaty of peace. An intelligent peace dictated by a spirit of genuine democracy might well restore the international economic coöperation that preceded the first World War and resulted in the progressive elevation of the standard of life in so many parts of the world. Even in the event of a democratic triumph complete freedom of trade is inconceivable, but freer trade nourished by wise governmental supervision is possible.

On the other hand, if the totalitarian powers should win, mutually beneficial economic coöperation will be impossible, since the raw materials and the markets of conquered countries, and perhaps of all others, will be integrated in the pattern of a new world order designed and managed for the special advantage of the victors. Regimented trade rather than comparative freedom of trade will prevail under such a regime.

Specifically, what can the United States do to safeguard the economic integrity of the Western Hemisphere in the changed world that is bound to emerge from the present conflict? We must help to restore Latin America's purchasing power, which has been so greatly reduced as a result of the war. There are many ways in which this can be done, but space permits a review of only a few of them here.

First, the encouragement of the production of rubber and tin. A large hemispheric supply of rubber and tin is good insurance in periods of international conflict, and could provide a foundation for a considerable amount of inter-American trade. The United States today consumes about 600,000 tons of natural rubber a year, which is more than half of the world's export of that product. We buy approximately 96 per cent of our crude rubber from the British, Dutch, and French Oriental tropics. Brazil founded the rubber industry, but, as we have seen, that industry migrated to Malaya, Indo-China, and the East Indies, from which now comes 90 per cent of the world's supply. Rubber is a rival of steel in modern civilization, and many of our greatest American industrial plants are completely dependent upon an adequate supply of it. Yet for most of our supply we must rely on the Dutch-British monopoly cartel. In a single year the United States pays $180,000,000 for Far Eastern and African rubber, but buys none from Brazil.

Development of rubber production in South America requires a long-term investment of funds; it will take from ten to twenty years to reëstablish the Brazilian rubber industry, but it would be a profitable enterprise and provide from

500,000 to 600,000 new jobs for native workers, thereby increasing purchasing power in impoverished areas. The manufacture of synthetic rubber in the United States is possible; indeed, significant progress has already been made in this direction; but the synthetic product costs from two to five times the current world prices for crude rubber. The Congress of the United States has already appropriated $500,000 to be spent under an agreement between the United States Department of Agriculture and eleven Latin American countries for research, experimentation, and the propagation of rubber trees. A number of American manufacturing companies have rubber-production concessions in South America. Mr. Henry Ford, for example, has a concession of over a million acres in the Amazon valley, where he hopes to develop an efficient, modern plantation.

The annual output of tin in the Bolivian mines is valued at $25,000,000. The United States buys twice that much but must haul it from Dutch and British mines in the Far East or from smelters in Great Britain and northern Europe. Eighty-five per cent of the entire output of the world's tin is in British hands. Thus the tin produced in Bolivian mines is shipped to Europe and then shipped back to the United States, a journey of 11,000 miles, a fact which causes delay and enhances the price.[18] The United States is taking steps to remedy this situation. The Reconstruction Finance Corporation announced on February 26, 1941, that a tin smelter would be built at Texas City, Texas, where Bolivian ores are to be refined.

Second, the purchase in Latin America of numerous other

---
[18] Carlton Beals, *Pan America,* p. 45.

products which the United States now buys elsewhere. Commodities such as cocoa, coconuts, quinine, tannin, numerous vegetable fibers, and even peanuts, of which this country is the world's largest consumer, are available or can readily be made so in Latin America. For example, the United States buys more than $50,000,000 worth of cocoa annually, yet Latin America has lost the major portion of its cocoa trade to Africa. South America is the native habitat of the quinine tree, the product of which is one of the most essential vegetable derivatives in curative medicine. For three centuries the Andean countries of Peru, Bolivia, Colombia, and Ecuador were the only sources of the world's supply of quinine. Today more than 90 per cent of all commercial quinine comes from Java, Sumatra, and the neighboring Oriental islands, where cheap labor, abundant capital, and well-managed plantations, planted with stock from Latin America, have made possible a Dutch monopoly in this important product. The United States is the world's largest importer and consumer of coconut products. The greatest of these is copra, the dried meat of the mature nut, from which are manufactured soaps, margarines, candies, cosmetics, perfumes, livestock feeds, and numerous other consumer goods. Brazilian coastal plains have about 2,000,000 coconut-bearing palms, yet practically no coconuts are exported. Ceylon provides the major portion of our billion pounds of imported copra each year.

Latin America is buying our automobiles, shoes, machinery, tractors, farm implements, ready-made clothing, electrical goods, and thousands of other items of merchandise, whereas Africa, Java, Borneo, French Indo-China, and British Malaya buy little from us. Increased purchases of commodities in Latin America would enable it to buy even more of our goods, thus resulting in mutually beneficial trade.[14]

Third, the provision of capital for the development of new industries in Latin America. A prosperous Latin America is the best guarantee of improved inter-American trade relations, and it is generally agreed among students of Pan-American economic life that increasing industrialization of South and Central America will do much to elevate the standard of living and increase purchasing power. In that development the United States is deeply interested. Not only the rubber industry, but many others, such as production of tin and other metals, the manufacture of iron and steel, and the refining of petroleum need development.

The United States is the only important source of the capital necessary to the development of new industries in Latin America. The policy which the United States has recently adopted, of making loans from government funds to encourage new industries in other American republics, may prove a very significant factor in the economic future of those countries. These loans are being made at reasonable rates of interest and for such long-term periods of repayment that the borrowers will have ample time in which to develop profitable industries, the output of which will repay the principal and interest. "Incidentally, one of the reasons why South America has had difficulties in paying back previous loans has been that the interest and financing charges were often so

---

[14] On the possibilities of inter-American trade see "Buy Hemisphere Products," by Charles Morrow Wilson, *Harpers Magazine,* January, 1941, pp. 147–155.

heavy that it would have been impossible for any industry in any country to pay back the loan, regardless of how effectively the money was used."[15] The new United States loans will not be characterized by such disadvantageous terms.

Fourth, the establishment of an Inter-American Bank. The provision of necessary capital and other steps required for the strengthening of Western Hemisphere economy may make imperative the organization of an Inter-American Bank. Such a bank would become the chief intergovernmental agency for stabilizing the economy and currency of Latin American nations. A considerable number of the American republics have already approved such an institution, and it undoubtedly will be sponsored by the United States. In fact, the organization of the bank awaits Senate ratification of the convention, and congressional authorization of the United States government's subscription in the institution, which is to have a minimum capital of $100,000,000. The Inter-American Bank plan grew out of the Panama Conference of American Foreign Ministers in 1939. Under the proposed charter, the bank would be empowered to help stabilize currencies, promote industrial development in the Americas, and otherwise advance the economic welfare of this hemisphere. It could grant loans or credits to governments or individuals and guarantee loans.

Such an institution would necessarily function in close collaboration with the American Export-Import Bank, which received a $500,000,000 authorization from Congress last year for assisting other American republics as an economic defense measure.

---

[15] Ezekiel, *op. cit.,* p. 133.

Fifth, the improvement of transportation facilities. Lack of transportation facilities has been recognized as one of the most serious obstacles to the economic development of Central and South America. These countries have been cut off from one another by high mountains or impassable swamps, jungles, or deserts. River or ocean transport has been the only feasible means of communication and travel. Valuable minerals and fertile plateaus have been left undeveloped because of inadequate means of communication and transportation. Lack of roads, railroads, and inter-American shipping has prevented exploitation. Europe seemed nearer to Latin America than was the United States, as of course it actually is between certain points. "Nearly the whole south continent lies east of New York, and the tip of Brazil, in longitude, is about 1800 miles nearer Europe. It is therefore closer to Africa and Europe than we are, closer to those two continents than to us."[16] Because European shipping facilities have been adequate, Latin American goods are often more easily transported to the markets of Europe than to those of the United States.

Progress is being made in the solution of the problem of communication and transportation. Airlines are creating accessibility through such companies as Pan-American Airways. The Inter-American Highway is an important project that will link North and South America. The Pan-American Highway will connect with the Inter-American Highway to facilitate travel through all the Americas. It costs several times as much to travel between New York and South America as

---

[16] Beals, *op. cit.,* p. 136.

between New York and Europe. To remedy that situation the United States Maritime Commission is granting subsidies and assistance to freight and passenger shipping lines. In times of peace European countries regard it a poor year if American tourists do not spend more than $80,000,000. When travel facilities are adequate a considerable proportion of this expenditure might be made in Latin America, thus aiding the expansion of inter-American trade.

Sixth, improvement in the standard of life. Permanent expansion of inter-American trade is not likely to be assured unless the United States, together with the governments of Central and South America, takes an active interest in the elevation of the standard of life for the great mass of Latin Americans, who not only have little voice in the public affairs of many of the constituent republics, so called, but whose impoverished status provides no effective demand for goods and services. The gulf between owners of wealth and the toiling masses is nowhere deeper and wider than it is in Latin America. Unfortunately, the eulogy of democratic ideals has seldom implemented itself in concrete movements for progressive improvement in the life of the masses of people. The South American continent is still predominantly an agricultural region, composed of great landowners and a vassal peasantry. The landowning class, which constitutes 7 per cent of the population, own almost all the land and control almost all the governments.[17] The landless peons, prototypes of the medieval serf, own no land, but till the master's land in return for the use of enough soil on which to raise their own subsist-

---
[17] Carr, *op. cit.*, p. 23.

ence. Often they receive no money wage, and are completely outside the money economy.[18] Impoverished and illiterate, democracy has no meaning for them, nor can they provide markets for trade expansion. Economic and social security is a pressing need in Latin America if the economic future of this hemisphere is to be as bright as it can be. If the United States is to spend its wealth lavishly in the economic development of Latin America, its investment in a Good Neighbor policy should have the assurance that all, and not merely a few, of the good neighbors shall share in the results.

A difficult task.—The task that lies before the United States is not an easy one, and wishful thinking about the future of inter-American trade will not create that trade. Many obstacles will appear to prevent the development of trade relations to their fullest possibilities. Realistic thinking is imperative, if our program is not to produce depressing disillusionment. In the first place, we must recognize that the agricultural interest of the United States, and many industrial interests, are not enthusiastic about a Pan-Americanism that calls for economic reciprocity. After all, the wheat and meat and corn of Argentina enter into direct competition with our own farm products, of which we have huge surpluses. The same is true of Brazilian cotton. When on April 1, 1941, the United States Senate passed a compromise measure allowing the Army and Navy to purchase 20,000,000 pounds of canned beef from Latin American countries, an amendment provided that this should be done only when domestic products of satisfactory quality should not be available. Our economic self-

---
[18] *Ibid.*

interest makes us eager to sell in every market of the world, but often we fail to recognize the elementary economic truth that our customers cannot continue to buy from us unless they can sell to us.

A second fact which realistic thinking will compel us to recognize is that in the postwar world Europe and Latin America must of necessity reëstablish trade relations. Europe normally buys 55 per cent of all Latin American exports, compared with our purchase of only 32 per cent. Latin America sold $125,000,000 worth of meat abroad in 1938. The United States imported $20,000,000 worth of meat specialties that year, but only $6,000,000 worth came from Latin America. It is reasonable to expect that, when the war ends, Europe will desire to supply her needs for foodstuffs and raw materials from the large surpluses of Latin America, and that Latin America, historically so closely identified with Europe, will wish to sell such surpluses in exchange for the things she needs.

The third thing which economic realism requires us to recognize is that there are but three ways in which our Latin American neighbors can pay for goods, namely, gold, goods, and credit. They have relatively little gold, because the United States possesses more than $20,000,000,000 of it, or fully 80 per cent of the world's supply. They find it difficult to pay for goods with goods, because our protective tariff is designed to keep out their merchandise. They can pay with credit, if the United States will extend the credit. The history of our investments in Central and South America does not lend too much encouragement in this direction, especially since the movement for the confiscation of foreign properties, so effectively initiated by Mexico, has become popular in many other countries. American investments in Latin America in the so-called new era of 1923–1929 reached an estimated total of $6,000,000,000, and repudiation of debts, together with defaults, left American investors holding the sack.[19]

Conclusion.—Other difficulties confront us in our program for inter-American trade in the postwar era, but enough has been said to indicate the magnitude of our task. Despite the economic limitations on good neighborliness, the same sense of reality that compels us to recognize these limitations may also force us to acknowledge that we do not live in a world in which economic considerations are the sole or determining ones in the behavior of individuals or nations. What may seem to be economically impossible or inexpedient may, under the irresistible pressure of necessity, become politically intelligent and socially expedient. The choice of alternatives is not always free. In the present chaotic state of the world and the inevitable dilemmas of the postwar reconstruction period this nation, like others, may find it imperative to do many things that defy traditional economic policy, at least until reason and sanity shall repossess the human mind and justice reinhabit the human heart.

If the war should end in a victory for the Axis, which at the moment seems much too possible to be comfortable, the Americas will face the most dangerous threat to their economic and political independence in their history. To preserve our freedom and our democratic institutions, we may

---

[19] Beals, *op. cit.*, p. 395.

find it necessary to construct economic defenses that will be quite untraditional.

Some months ago, Dr. Walter Funk, economics minister of the German Third Reich, warned the Americas that the new Europe dominated by Germany will trade with the countries of the Western Hemisphere only on German terms and under German-dictated arrangements. A few weeks later, the voice of Dr. Funk's master, Adolph Hitler, raucously bellowed to the workers in a Berlin munitions factory these words: "We find ourselves amid a controversy which aims at more than the victory of one or another country. In fact, it is a struggle between two worlds.... Two worlds are in conflict, two philosophies of life.... One of these worlds must break asunder."

The world of which Herr Hitler dreams and which it is the duty of Herr Funk to plan is a world of closed economic empires; it involves the creation of spheres of commercial and cultural influence stemming from Berlin, Rome, and Tokyo and dominated by the Axis. In that new world conventional economic practices will give way to rigid national controls, direct barter, and blocked currencies, in which the union of economics and politics will destroy freedom of individual enterprise and action.

It is obvious that, if Germany wins the war, the Americas will face a hostile new order—an order of arrogant militarism, insatiable imperialism, and denial of independent sovereignty; an order in which international affairs and relations will be organized on the costly basis of armed peace and recurrent wars. To the peoples of the Western Hemisphere that new order of things will constitute a most serious menace to their collective security and prosperity. If the democratic tradition possesses the values which its champions claim for it, the United States may find it imperative to safeguard those values, not only for its own future generations, but for future generations of good neighbors to the south as well.

THE INFLUENCE OF THE WAR ON THE AGRICULTURE OF THE AMERICAS

HARRY R. WELLMAN
PROFESSOR OF AGRICULTURAL ECONOMICS
IN THE UNIVERSITY OF CALIFORNIA

Lecture delivered April 22, 1941

THE INFLUENCE OF THE WAR ON THE AGRICULTURE OF THE AMERICAS

SHORTLY after Germany gained virtual control of continental Europe early last summer, we began to get reports of the slaughter of livestock in Denmark and the Netherlands. Recently we have been hearing about the burning of corn in Argentina. These two incidents, although separated by more than 6000 nautical miles in distance and by several months in time, are closely related. Slaughter of breeding herds in Denmark and the Netherlands after the German invasion was not caused fundamentally by an urgent need of the Germans for meat, nor was it undertaken by the Danish and Dutch farmers in retaliation. Rather was it done because of the shortage of feed. Corn is being burned in Argentina not because of its superior quality as a fuel, but because of the absence of livestock to eat it. The livestock that needs the corn is on the continent of Europe, the corn that the livestock needs is in Argentina, and the two are being kept apart by the war.

Argentina is the world's largest exporter of corn, accounting on the average for nearly two-thirds of all corn shipped in international trade. Western European countries are the chief importers of corn. Continental Europe normally takes over one-half of the world's corn exports, and the United Kingdom normally takes one-third.

Although the continent of Europe is a net exporter of livestock products, chiefly from Denmark and The Netherlands to the United Kingdom, those countries do not produce a sufficient amount of feed for the number of animals they normally raise, and hence must purchase large quantities of concentrates—feed grains, oil cake, and meal—from overseas.[1] When overseas supplies of such feeds are cut off or greatly curtailed, farmers have only two alternatives: to kill some of their livestock, or to permit them to starve. The former is the lesser of the two evils. So throughout western Europe today, and particularly in Denmark, The Netherlands, and France, livestock numbers are being drastically reduced.

Even Britain is experiencing an acute shortage of feed, owing to the destruction of shipping. On March 19, 1941, the British minister of agriculture announced that it would be necessary to curtail existing feed rations for farm animals and that an appreciable number of livestock would have to be slaughtered.

Argentina is one of the chief livestock-producing countries of the world and is the largest exporter of meat and meat products, accounting on the average for nearly one-third of the world's exports of these items. The question may well be raised, Why does not Argentina feed her corn to her livestock instead of burning it? The answer is that in Argentina grass is a cheaper feed than corn for cattle and sheep, which are the most important kinds of livestock raised there, almost irrespective of how low in price corn gets. The Grain Board of Argentina has purchased large quantities of 1940 crop corn from farmers at around 20 cents a bushel and has offered it

---

[1] P. Lamartine Yates, *Food Production in Western Europe* (London, 1940).

for sale to livestock producers at 5 cents a bushel, but has found few takers. Livestock producers with an abundance of grass which, if not used, would go to waste are not inclined to lay out cash money, however little, for feed, and particularly in view of the fact that the livestock industry itself is depressed by reason of loss of export outlets. Argentina's exports of beef in 1940 were about 30 per cent smaller than in 1939 and about 15 per cent smaller than the 1936-1938 average. With Argentine exports of corn drastically curtailed, and with little demand for it on the part of the domestic livestock producers, much of the 1940 crop is still stored in open cribs, where it is subject to heavy spoilage. The 1941 crop now ready for harvest promises to be the largest on record, and the present outlook for its disposal is far from encouraging. Is it any wonder, then, that Argentina is experimenting with the use of corn for fuel in power plants and factories?

In the case of Argentine corn we have perhaps the most drastic adverse effects of World War II on the various agricultural products of the Americas. But I suspect that diligent search would uncover other products that are being harmed almost as much by the loss of export outlets. In our own state of California we have one such example, namely, Hardy pears, which are produced mainly in Santa Clara County. In the years preceding this war, about 90 per cent of the Hardy pear crop of the State was exported, almost entirely to the United Kingdom. Since November, 1939, Britain has prohibited the importation of fresh pears from non-Empire sources. Two things prevented the greater part of the 1940 Hardy pear crop from being left to rot on the ground. Canners purchased a large tonnage for manufacture into fruit cocktail (but at a very low price), and the Federal Surplus Marketing Administration purchased about the same tonnage for distribution to persons on relief. Total returns to growers failed by a considerable margin to cover their costs of production and harvesting, and of those total returns 60 per cent was derived from the sale of pears to the Federal government.

Argentine corn and California Hardy pears are, as I have indicated, extreme cases. Most of the farm products of the Americas have suffered much less during this war than have those two commodities. Some farm products have experienced no adverse effects, and others have actually been benefited. But for farm products of the Western Hemisphere in the aggregate, the meaning of this war to date has been loss of markets.

Before discussing the happenings of the past twenty months, it would be well to fix in our minds some outstanding characteristics of the agriculture of the Americas.

First, we should mention the fact that agriculture is of large importance in the economy of all the countries in the Americas—North and South—and that in many of them the raising of crops and livestock overshadows all other activities. About two-thirds of the people in the twenty Latin American republics, one-third of the people in Canada, and one-fourth of the people in this country are engaged directly in agricultural pursuits.

One of the characteristics which many of the countries in the Western Hemisphere have in common is the predominance of agricultural products in their export trade. Exports from the six Central American countries, from the three West Indian republics, and from four of the ten South American countries—Argentina, Brazil, Paraguay, and Uruguay—consist almost entirely of agricultural products. In addition, about three-fourths of the exports of Colombia and about two-thirds of the exports of Ecuador are agricultural products. Peru exports slightly more mineral than agricultural products, while the exports from Bolivia, Chile, and Venezuela consist largely of mineral products. Mexico also exports mainly mineral products.

In the foreign trade of the twenty Latin American republics, two features stand out clearly: first, the exports of each of them consist in large part or entirely of raw materials, agricultural and mineral; and second, the imports of each of them consist chiefly of manufactured products.[2] The composition of Canada's foreign trade is similar to that of the Latin American countries, although the relative importance of raw materials in her export trade and of manufactured goods in her import trade are not so great.

In sharp contrast to the general character of the foreign trade of the other countries in the Western Hemisphere, three-fourths of the total exports of the United States consist of manufactured products, and only one-fourth consists of raw materials. While this country is a large exporter of agricultural products, both raw and manufactured, the value of such exports in recent years has amounted to only 25 per cent of the total value of all our exports. On the other hand, more

---

[2] U. S. Tariff Commission, *The Foreign Trade of Latin America* (in three parts) (Washington, D. C., 1940).

The Meaning of the War

than 50 per cent of our total imports by value are agricultural products. About one-half of our agricultural imports are competitive with products grown commercially in this country, and the other half consist of complementary products which we do not produce commercially, such as rubber, coffee, raw silk, cacao beans, wool for carpets, bananas, tea, and spices.

Taken together, the countries in the Western Hemisphere are large net exporters of agricultural products. In addition to their own requirements, the Americas, all together, produce large surpluses of grains, meats, fruits, fibers, coffee, and tobacco.[3] Canada ranks first among the countries of the world in the exports of wheat; the United States in the exports of cotton, tobacco, pork products, and fruits; Cuba in the exports of sugar; Brazil in the exports of coffee; and Argentina in the exports of beef, corn, and flaxseed. In addition, Argentina ranks second in the exports of both wheat and wool. The Caribbean countries together furnish over two-thirds of the world's exports of bananas.

The flow of agricultural exports from countries in the Western Hemisphere forms two great streams, one of which empties into Europe and the other into the United States. Exports of agricultural products from the Americas to Asia, Africa, and Oceania are relatively insignificant. Also, inter-American trade in agricultural products, except to the United States, is of minor importance. Each of the Latin American countries and Canada normally ship more agricultural products to the United States than to all other countries in the Western Hemi-

[3] Joseph L. Apodaca, "Agriculture's Role in Hemisphere Defense," U. S. Dept. Agr., *Foreign Agriculture*, March, 1941.

Wellman: Agriculture

sphere combined. We export some agricultural products to Canada and to the Latin American countries, but in the aggregate such exports are small as compared with those to Europe.[4]

The reasons for the small imports of agricultural products into the Latin American countries stem in part from their varied agriculture and in part from the low standards of living and restricted diets of the masses of the people. Within most of the Latin American countries, including those that lie wholly between the Tropic of Cancer and the Tropic of Capricorn, the variations in climate are such as to permit the growing of a rather wide range of products. Large areas of several of the tropical countries are at considerable elevations, and there temperate-zone types of products are grown for domestic consumption. I do not wish to imply that sufficient quantities of every kind of foodstuff needed for a balanced diet are produced in those countries. Far from it. A considerable proportion of the 123 million people in Latin America are undernourished. In this country, too, many people are ill fed, ill clothed, and ill housed, but not nearly to the degree that they are in the countries to the south.

[4] In 1937 the Latin American countries shipped 32 per cent of their agricultural exports to the United States and 56 per cent to Europe. Only 9 per cent were taken by themselves and Canada and only 3 per cent by all other countries. In the same year about 70 per cent of Canada's exports of agricultural products went to Europe, mainly to the United Kingdom, while about 20 per cent came to this country. The other 10 per cent were about equally divided between the Latin American countries on the one hand and the countries in Africa, Asia, and Oceania on the other. About 70 per cent of our exports of agricultural products in 1937 went to Europe, 7 per cent to Canada, 8 per cent to the Latin American countries, and 17 per cent to other countries, chiefly Japan, which in that year was a heavy purchaser of our cotton.

96 The Meaning of the War

In order to complete this very general background picture, we now need to turn our attention to Europe, which has always been the chief market for the agricultural exports of the Americas. Europe is a large net importer of foodstuffs and fibers.[5] Although many countries in Europe are themselves important producers of agricultural commodities, the aggregate production in Europe is not sufficient to meet the needs of the population, despite the fact that several of the countries, such as Italy, Germany, and France, have made strenuous efforts during the past decade to become self-sufficient in foodstuffs.

As far as markets for the agricultural products of the Western Hemisphere are concerned, we need to distinguish between the continental European countries on the one hand and the British Isles on the other. The former are at the present time in large part closed to overseas shipments, while the latter are not. As a net importer of foodstuffs and closely related items, the United Kingdom is of far greater importance than all the countries on the continent of Europe combined. In 1935, for example, the United Kingdom accounted for 70 per cent of the total European imports of food while conti-

---

[5] In 1935 Europe's recorded import balance of foodstuffs amounted to 1720 million dollars and her import balance of fibers, mainly wool and cotton, amounted to 1076 million dollars. In addition, her net imports of tobacco amounted to 128 million dollars. These three sums, totaling 2824 million dollars, do not, however, tell the entire story. Europe also imports large quantities of oil seeds, cake, and meal for livestock feeding and considerable amounts of fertilizers, such as raw phosphates, for the production of domestic vegetable crops. The value of these imports in 1935 together with that of whale oil amounted to 418 million dollars, bringing the total import balance of foodstuffs, fibers, and closely related items up to $3\frac{1}{8}$ billion dollars. See *Europe's Trade*, League of Nations publication, 1941.

nental Europe accounted for only 30 per cent. With respect to fibers, however, just the reverse situation prevailed; continental Europe took 70 per cent of the total and the United Kingdom 30 per cent.

Although the United Kingdom is a larger net importer of agricultural products than the continent of Europe, the Latin American countries are more dependent upon continental Europe than upon the United Kingdom as an outlet for their products. In 1937, for example, about 37 per cent of the total exports of the twenty Latin American countries went to the continent of Europe as against 19 per cent to the United Kingdom. In the same year, United States exports of agricultural products to Europe were about equally divided between the continent and the United Kingdom. On the other hand, virtually all of Canada's agricultural exports to Europe went to the United Kingdom.

The story of agricultural exports from the Americas to Europe during the course of this war to date falls into two fairly distinct chapters; the first from September, 1939, through April, 1940, and the second from May, 1940, to April, 1941. Perhaps this month will see the close of the second chapter and the beginning of a third.

This story might well be centered about the agricultural exports from the United States, one reason being that we have more information about the exports of our own country than about those of our neighbors. Certain major developments in the agricultural exports of other American countries, however, will be brought into the picture.

During the first eight months of this war, the total United

States exports of agricultural products, exclusive of cotton, averaged 4 per cent above the 1934-1938 level. Cotton exports were 37 per cent greater, owing largely to the very small takings in the previous year and the abnormally heavy purchases by Russia. Direct exports to Germany ceased from the very start of the war, as did also direct exports to Austria and Czechoslovakia, which Germany had already taken over, and to Poland, which she quickly conquered. This immediate loss, however, was not a particularly serious one so far as foreign outlets for United States agricultural products were concerned, as with Hitler's rise to power we had already lost most of the German market. Brazil's immediate loss was relatively much more serious than our own. In 1938, for example, Germany took nearly 20 per cent of Brazil's agricultural exports, as compared with less than 5 per cent of ours.

At the outbreak of this war, it was quite generally assumed that there would be a marked pickup in European demand for many of our farm products, and for a brief period prices of numerous items advanced sharply. But the expected increase in demand failed to materialize and the temporary flurry in prices quietly subsided. During the first year of World War I, 1914-15, our exports of foodstuffs were nearly twice as large as the average of the previous five years, but during the comparable period of this war scarcely any increase was realized.

The reasons for the relatively small exports of agricultural products from this country during the period September, 1939, to April, 1940, are many and varied. I will mention only those which seem to me to be the more important ones.

Outstanding among these reasons was the policy of Great Britain and France designed to conserve their available dollar exchange for the purchase of war materials which they could not obtain elsewhere. Since our neutrality legislation provided that countries at war must pay cash for all their purchases from us, it is easy to understand why Britain and France turned to countries where similar restrictions were not in force for such items as could be obtained from them. Thus while our exports of wheat in 1939-40 were only one half as large as the average of the two previous years, Argentina's exports were nearly twice as large.

Britain and France also found it desirable to take the exportable surpluses of their dominions and colonies in order to cement their empires. These purchases consisted mainly of agricultural products. Still another factor in the situation was the purchase by the Allies of agricultural products from the Balkan countries and Turkey, with the twofold purpose of preventing the sale of products to Germany and of obtaining possible allies or at least friendly neutrals. Under the British-French agreement with Turkey, for example, the allied nations bound themselves to purchase annually until March, 1943, huge quantities of Turkish raisins and tobacco. Purchases under this agreement largely accounted for the early decline in our exports of these items.

The second chapter of the export story might well begin with Germany's invasion of Norway twelve and a half months ago. Up to that time there was little actual combat, but from then until the middle of June events moved with unbelievable rapidity. With the fall of France and Italy's entry into the war, Britain extended her blockade to include virtually the entire continent of Europe, thus almost completely closing off that area as a market for Western Hemisphere products. This is a distinct contrast to the situation that existed in the second year of World War I. Recall briefly the alignment in Europe at that time. On the side of the Central Powers were Germany, Austria-Hungary, Bulgaria, and Turkey. Against the Central Powers were Great Britain, France, Russia, Belgium, Serbia, and Italy. In 1916 the Allies were joined by Rumania, Greece, and Portugal. The neutrals in Europe consisted of Sweden, Norway, Denmark, The Netherlands, Spain, and Switzerland. At no time during the first World War were we excluded from exporting to the allied and neutral countries, and there were many of them. But not so today.

The virtual closure of the continental European markets last summer fell heavily upon the agricultural exporting countries of the Americas, such as Argentina, Brazil, Ecuador, Uruguay, Paraguay, and the United States. In the years just prior to this war, each of these countries had sent from one-third to one-half of their total exports of agricultural products to the continent of Europe. It is a serious thing to lose even 10 per cent of one's markets, while to be deprived of one-third or more may well be ruinous.

Beginning in April, 1940, United States exports of every important group of agricultural products fell precipitously. Average exports of all agricultural products during the last half of 1940 amounted to only 29 million dollars a month as against an average of 78 million dollars a month during the period September, 1939, to April, 1940, a decrease of 63 per cent. Not only were our exports to continental Europe almost completely cut off, but also our exports to the United Kingdom were drastically curtailed. During the last six months of 1940 our average monthly exports of agricultural products to the United Kingdom amounted to only 8 million dollars as against 23 million dollars a month during the first seven months of this war, a decrease of 65 per cent.

The British blockade explains our loss of exports to the continent of Europe but does not, of course, account for the great shrinkage in our exports of agricultural products to the United Kingdom herself. With her access to supplies from the continent cut off, Britain was forced to extend her trade routes and at the same time was subjected to greater shipping hazards from German submarines and bombers. Her dollar exchange situation also was made more stringent than before by reason of the loss of French credits and the need for increasing her purchases of war materials in this country. Under the necessity of economizing on both ocean cargo space and dollar exchange, it is easy to see why Britain felt she must reduce her purchase of agricultural products in this country to a minimum.

This month of April, 1941, may well mark the beginning of the third chapter of the story of agricultural exports from the Americas, but what it will unfold no man can foretell. There is little question about the grave need of food in Europe. Hunger is one of the specters haunting large numbers of people across the Atlantic, while on this side surpluses of certain foodstuffs bear heavily upon the farmers. The available evidence suggests that the food situation in the British

Isles is becoming acute, if it has not already reached that stage, while in the invaded countries on the Continent large numbers of people are probably close to starvation. But whether the Americas can or will send their surpluses of foodstuffs abroad depends very largely upon the future development of this war.

One of the major obstacles to Britain's imports of agricultural products from the United States, namely, the lack of dollar exchange, was removed with the passage of the Lend-Lease Bill last month. But the other major obstacle, lack of transportation, still remains. Until the British shipping situation is eased, and it may get worse before it gets better, only the bare minimum of cargo space will probably be used for carrying foodstuffs. Nations at war can skimp on food, but not on munitions. Lack of proper diet may slowly weaken a people; lack of adequate war materials may spell quick defeat.

Even though the total food imports of the United Kingdom remain at a low level, shipments from this country will probably increase during the coming months, assuming, of course, that Britain stands. Continued heavy losses of shipping will force Britain to shorten and concentrate her trade routes. Less of her food imports would then come from distant Empire countries such as Australia, New Zealand, and the Union of South Africa, and more would come from the Americas, particularly Canada and the United States. Already New Zealand is being plagued with large stocks of meat and butter accumulating in storage for want of shipping space to the United Kingdom.

The losses of British and neutral shipping in March, 1941, amounting to about 400,000 tons, were somewhat larger than in January, 1917, but still considerably below the average of the succeeding six months. As many of you will recall, the "all out" German submarine attack of the first World War began in the late summer of 1916. Destruction of shipping, which in the previous year had been running around 150,000 tons a month, climbed rapidly during that fall and winter and in April, 1917, reached the staggering total of 850,000 tons. It is said that the British Isles were down to three weeks' supply of numerous important foodstuffs during the height of the submarine attack in 1917.

As their shipping losses began to mount during the first World War, the Allies turned more and more to North America for their needs and soon were bidding frantically for foodstuffs here while supplies in more distant countries went begging. Exports of wheat, for example, from both Argentina and Australia declined markedly during World War I, while from Canada and the United States they greatly increased.

Even though Britain should from now on in this war obtain a larger proportion of her food imports from the United States and Canada, there is little danger of any immediate shortage of most supplies for domestic consumption here. Of wheat, for example, Canada had on hand on March 1, 1941, an exportable surplus great enough to take care of the entire import requirements of the United Kingdom for about three years. In addition, the United States has excess supplies of wheat great enough to carry England for another two years.

Thus, if the English should want for bread, it will be on account of shortage of transportation rather than of any lack of supplies of wheat available for export from North America.

Many other foodstuffs such as edible fats, beans, and fruits are also available in ample quantities in this country for export to the United Kingdom. We also have abundant supplies of feed grains and hay, and could step up livestock production appreciably. The United States Department of Agriculture has recently established minimum prices on eggs, butter, and hogs, with a view to encouraging their production. It may be that Britain will want more pork, dairy, and poultry products during the next few months than we can readily supply from our present production. During the first World War she was able to fill a part of her need for these items from Denmark and the Netherlands, but she cannot do so now.

The continent of Europe still remains largely closed to the agricultural products of the Americas. How soon and to what extent foodstuffs will be sent to the peoples of the invaded countries on the Continent, which would relieve their hunger and at the same time ease our depressed markets, will, I suppose, depend largely upon war strategy. We have great sympathy for the unfortunates of Europe, and we have a keen interest in restoring prices to our own farmers, but these considerations may have to give way to the more urgent need of defeating Hitler. Britain is in the throes of a life-and-death struggle. She cannot well afford to permit imports into the conquered countries even to relieve the suffering of innocent people, if such imports would in any respect strengthen the Axis powers. And we, too, are likely to refrain from any action, however meritorious in itself, that has the possibility of making Britain's task more difficult.

Thus far we have been discussing the effects of the war upon the European demand for Western Hemisphere farm products. But there is another side to the picture, and that is its influence on the demand for agricultural commodities on this side of the Atlantic, particularly in the United States. What happens to the demand of consumers in this country is of great importance, not only to our own farmers, but also to those of other countries in this hemisphere, and especially those in the Caribbean countries. During recent years more than 90 per cent of our total production of agricultural products has been consumed in this country, and in addition the United States has provided a market for about 85 per cent of the agricultural exports of the Caribbean countries. We also take over half of Brazil's coffee exports, although we do not take any of her cotton, which is her second most important export crop. For Argentina, however, this country has never been an important market. True, we take some of her flaxseed, canned beef, cattle hides, carpet wool, and a few other items, but in the aggregate Argentina's shipments to this country have been small, constituting on the average only about 10 per cent of her total exports. Uruguay and Paraguay are in much the same position as Argentina as far as markets in the United States are concerned. These three countries, lying almost entirely in the temperate zone, produce about the same kind of agricultural commodities as we do ourselves.

This similarity of products constitutes perhaps the most serious obstacle to Western Hemisphere solidarity. Economically, the temperate-zone countries of South America are tied to Europe. That is where their markets are. We can and do take most of the agricultural exports of the Caribbean countries, and we could even increase materially our imports of numerous tropical products from that area if supplies there were available. But we do not and we cannot well take any large part of the exportable surpluses of temperate-zone products from the lower tier of countries in South America.

Argentina, for example, normally exports from one-third to one-half of her total production of meat products—beef, pork, and mutton,—from 60 to 80 per cent of her grain production—wheat and corn,—and around 90 per cent of her production of both flaxseed and wool. These commodities are also grown extensively in the United States, and the production of some of them normally exceeds our domestic requirements.

In order for the United States to afford a market for the exportable surpluses of Argentina and similar countries, it would be necessary to curtail drastically our own production of agricultural commodities. Such downward adjustment in the agriculture of this country would entail not only extremely serious economic problems, but very acute social problems as well. But unless the United States does take the products of those countries, they will be forced to trade with whichever power dominates Europe. Otherwise they face collapse.

In the long run the countries of South America could lessen materially their dependence on Europe through the expansion of domestic industries, with perhaps considerable advantage to themselves. Argentina has already started to do so and may be expected to continue. Such changes, however, cannot ordinarily be brought about quickly; many years are usually required. In the meantime those countries must have foreign markets. Perhaps the lesser of two evils would be for the United States to assist in maintaining the kind of Europe with which the South American countries as well as ourselves can trade without jeopardizing our security, rather than to take or underwrite their exportable surpluses.

Events of the past two years have made the United States a better market, at least temporarily, for those agricultural products which we normally import as well as for those grown in this country. Recovery from the 1937–38 depression had already set in before the outbreak of war in September, 1939, and this recovery was accelerated as manufacture of war materials for Britain and France got under way. Still further impetus to recovery was given by our own defense program, which has not yet reached its full stride. As compared with August, 1939, all indices relating to industrial activity and income payments are now materially higher: employment has increased, wages have risen, and consumers in this country have more money to spend.

Numerous analyses which have been made afford convincing evidence that increases in the money incomes of consumers in this country are accompanied by increases in demand for many items of food, particularly for milk, eggs, meat, fruits, and leafy vegetables. Such increase in demand, however, need not appear in the form of higher prices to farmers; instead it may appear in the form of larger quantities taken. This latter situation seems to have obtained for most agricultural products during 1940. With generally good yields in this country, together with the loss of exports, supplies available for the domestic market were so abundant that prices of most farm products were kept from rising. There are, of course, a number of exceptions to this generalization. Wool is one. Under the stimulus of government purchases for military purposes—uniforms and blankets—prices of wool advanced markedly during last fall and winter. For all groups of farm products, however, the index of prices at the end of 1940 was 6 per cent below the 1934–1938 average. Some small advances in farm prices were registered during the first quarter of this year, chiefly in meat animals, but in the main, prices of agricultural products in this country are still comparatively low.

I should like now to turn back to World War I and review briefly some of the salient points regarding the effects of that conflict on the agriculture of the Americas, with particular reference to the United States. During the first year of that war, 1914–15, prices of United States farm products as a group rose not at all, and it was not until the summer of 1916 that the real advance began, the same time as the "all out" German submarine attack started. Further impetus to price increases was given by our entry into that war in April, 1917. By the time of the signing of the Armistice in November, 1918, the index of farm prices in this country was at 205 as compared with 100 during the five years 1910–1914. But instead of turning down immediately thereafter, prices of farm products as well as prices of nearly everything else continued to rise during 1919 and the first half of 1920. In May, 1920, the index of farm prices was about 40 points above the high level of November, 1918.

The year 1919-20 saw not only the highest prices of farm products in the United States, but also our largest exports. It seemed in the year and a half following the Armistice that the accumulated shortages of foodstuffs and other materials in Europe could never be made up. There was frantic bidding for all kinds of goods. "The food ministries of European countries bought even more wildly than did individual consumers."[6] These purchases were financed largely by huge credits granted by this country.

Other countries in the Western Hemisphere as well as the United States benefited materially by the greatly enlarged demand for agricultural products in Europe. Ships were again free to carry the products of distant lands, and luxury-type foods as well as common necessities were taken. Coffee stocks which had been accumulating in Brazil for want of markets were released. Prices of coffee, which had averaged lower during the war than in the previous five years, almost doubled overnight. Exports of coffee from Brazil were 75 per cent larger in 1919 than in 1918.

In the United States, the four years 1916-17 through 1919-20 were the most prosperous period that farmers generally had known for several generations. While costs of production went up, they did not rise so fast as the prices of the products farmers produced. But this period of prosperity was short lived. The bubble burst in 1920.

In response to the high prices during the war and the months immediately following, and encouraged by the patriotic ap-

---

[6] A. B. Genung, "Agriculture in the World War Period," U. S. Dept. Agr. *Yearbook of Agriculture*, 1940.

peal, "Food will win the war," farmers in this country greatly expanded their production. About 40 million acres of grassland that had never before been broken were put under the plow. Expansion of agricultural production also occurred in other parts of the world—in Canada, Argentina, and Australia. In the aggregate the increase in the world's agricultural plant was substantial.

But as soon as the accumulated shortages in Europe were made up, the demand for the agricultural products of these newly expanded areas fell sharply. Moreover, normal production of foodstuffs in the European countries was gradually resumed, and several of them went even farther in expanding their domestic production as a means of reducing their dependence on outside sources.[7]

Farmers in this country found their export outlets curtailed from still another cause. The United States entered the first World War as a debtor nation; it emerged from that war as a creditor nation. Much of the capital used to build this country was borrowed from Europe, and we paid interest and principal in considerable part by exporting farm products. But with the change in our position from that of a debtor to that of a creditor, Europe could continue to buy our goods only if we extended her still more and more credit or took her goods in return. We tried the first for a while, but eventually found it to be a "dead end" street. We have persistently refused to adopt the second course.

It is not, I think, an exaggeration to say that in this country

---

[7] L. B. Bacon and F. C. Schloemer, "World Trade in Agricultural Products," Internat. Inst. Agr., 1940.

gains to farmers in the first World War were largely wiped out during the early 1920's. Particularly in the Middle West, many farmers had gone heavily into debt for land and equipment purchased at wartime values. When prices tumbled in 1920-21, they found themselves with a greatly increased debt burden and a drastically reduced income.

To an appreciable degree, the first World War left the agriculture of the United States with an overextended plant and an unbalanced structure. Thus, it was rendered particularly vulnerable to the series of shocks which occurred during the past two decades: the drastic curtailment of export outlets; the substitution of mechanical for horse power on the farms, which in itself released about 30 million acres for additional production for market; and finally, the sharp reduction in domestic demand that accompanied the severe depression of the early 1930's.

There is one consequence of World War I which has been late in appearing, but which nevertheless is a serious one. The wartime plow-up of 40 million acres of grassland has been extremely costly. Out of it, for example, came the Dust Bowl, which in turn contributed to mass migration of destitute farm families, many of whom came to California only to wander hopelessly up and down the state looking for jobs that did not exist.

I have given this brief and inadequate résumé of the aftermath of the first World War with respect to our agriculture, not because the identical pattern will be repeated this time—it will certainly be different in some respects,— but simply to remind you that the longer-run consequences of a war may be quite different from the immediate effects.

The Meaning of the War

Thus far in this war, total exports of agricultural products from the Western Hemisphere to Europe have been curtailed, and nowhere has the reduction been more pronounced than in the United States. In the comparable period of World War I, agricultural exports from the Western Hemisphere increased substantially and a large part of that increase accrued to the United States. At that time we obtained a "larger slice of a bigger pie." To date in this war we have had to accept a "smaller slice of a reduced pie." Currently the situation is changing in favor of larger agricultural exports from the United States, both absolutely and relatively. On this side of the Atlantic the rise in incomes of consumers in the United States has made this country a better market, not only for our own farm products, but for those of several of our neighbors as well. The reduction in exports to Europe, on the one hand, and the increase in United States demand, on the other, have affected very unevenly the different agricultural commodities produced in the Western Hemisphere. The position of some products has been materially improved while the position of others has been greatly weakened. The over-all effect, however, up to this time has been unfavorable.

Just how the agriculture of the United States and other countries in the Western Hemisphere will be influenced by this war during the months and years ahead, no one can predict with any confidence. It will depend upon many complex factors, which at this time we can see only vaguely or not at all. Will this country enter the war as an active belligerent? Can inflation of prices be avoided? Will the conflict be short or long? Will the Allied or the Axis nations be victorious?

In order to gain security from aggression will we have to maintain permanently a two- or three-ocean navy and a large air force and standing army, and if so, what will it mean to our standard of living? Will the United States again grant large credits to European nations for rehabilitation after the war is over? Will the nations of the world, including our own, move in the direction of freer international trade, or will they resume the nationalistic policies so prevalent during the 1930's?

POLITICS: THE OLD ORDER AND THE NEW

PAUL PÉRIGORD
PROFESSOR OF FRENCH CIVILIZATION IN THE UNIVERSITY OF CALIFORNIA

Lecture delivered April 29, 1941

POLITICS: THE OLD ORDER AND THE NEW

An adequate treatment of present American political problems raised by the unexpected and triumphant emergence of totalitarian powers should be prefaced by an outline, no matter how concise, of the geography, ethnology, and economics of the Western Hemisphere. For the sake of brevity, I must assume that my readers are familiar with the abundant and enlightening data supplied by my colleagues in the preceding lectures of this series. Even in the field assigned to me, I shall have to limit myself rigidly, as this world conflict produces different reactions in different countries and I could not examine them all. I propose, therefore, to study the impact of the present struggle for world domination first upon the United States, and then consider it in relation to the political independence and security of the Western Hemisphere.[1]

The politics of the Americas cannot be studied or understood except as a part of world politics. In order to be able to describe whither we are going, it is important to know where we are and whence we came. We should, therefore, recall briefly the foundations of a world which we had come to accept as our heritage. The post-Napoleonic world, itself a synthesis of the driving forces of the American, the French, and the Industrial revolutions, rested upon four major foundations: it was a world of nation-states, either fully achieved

---

[1] I wish gratefully to acknowledge in the preparation of this address the valuable and generous coöperation of Professor Malbone W. Graham, of the Department of Political Science in the University of California.

like France or Great Britain, or coming into being like Germany and Italy; it was a world characterized by the gradual spread of political liberty, liberty proceeding by leaps and bounds as in France, or slowly and laboriously as in Austria; it was a world economically organized around the principles of international exchange and open competition with a greater or lesser amount of free trade; it was a world policed by dominant British sea power. The navy of Great Britain, operating from widely scattered bases, watched the far reaches of the Atlantic and the Pacific. The United States assisted in that police duty. It grew strong and rich, and the Latin American nations developed to their present importance, while a military balance of power in Europe and the naval paramountcy of the British fleet assured a measure of world stability.

This world the destruction of which we are so tragically witnessing reached its full maturity at the close of the first World War, but it soon began to suffer dissolution, as one by one its foundations were removed: it ceased to be a world of relatively free trade and open competition, which were replaced by autarchy, that is, national or regional self-sufficiency; it ceased to be governed, in consequence, by the principles of liberty; it ceased to be policed by the naval forces of a single empire, the growth of competitive naval armaments limiting the freedom-maintenance role of British sea power; finally, with the advent of totalitarian regimes, it ceased to be a world of nation-states, and reverted to the imperial pattern, but conceived in a fundamentally new way, thus seemingly justifying the Nazi claim of a "new order."

This "new order," whether occurring in Asia, Africa, or

Périgord: Politics 119

Europe, revealed the following characteristics: a military mechanism, furnishing the leverage wherewith to displace the older constitutional and international legal structures and providing the elemental machinery of repression; an economic frame designed to organize life around new social forms; a monopolistic political system, fashioned to serve exclusively the ends of a given class or party or race; a system of society conceived for and dedicated to production of soldiers; a substitute religion, based on the diffusion, by a self-appointed elite, of destructive and appropriately manufactured myths, opposing to Christianity a new fanatical faith, commanding the utter devotion of its subjects and endowed with a terrifying efficiency.

Collectively taken, these five aspects of the German "new order" purpose to refashion the world to the exclusion of human individuality and freedom. Together they constitute a challenge which the United States of America is compelled to meet, for Hitler speaks of his desire to establish a new order which would assure to Europe or to the world "peace for a thousand years." To that end the coöperation required of us in both political and economic realms would be a matter of compulsion, with the lash applied by Germans as the dominant master race.

This plan, which until recently evoked the sneers of many, is being rapidly carried out, and now is awakening consternation. The friends of liberty must therefore think clearly and fast. We are beginning to realize that we shall be pushed aside unless we can demonstrate that democracy can be as active and dynamic a creed as any the Nazis possess. In order to do that, it is not necessary to have a revolution; for the strength of democracy is that it has found it possible to combine progress with popular consent. There is no need of abandoning a method which has served us so well. But we must increase the tempo of democracy, make it as dynamic in its action and as attractive in its appeal as the doctrines of violence.

We may detest the solution that Hitler and Stalin have found for the problem of the relation between the individual and the state. But does not our own need refreshing? It still rests upon the great advance of a century and a half ago, when the political rights of the citizen were finally codified and established in America by the Declaration of Independence, in France by the Revolution, and in Great Britain by the era of reform. Has not the time come to go farther? The citizens of a democracy should be guaranteed not merely their political liberties, but also the economic minimum without which the pursuit of happiness is merely an empty phrase.

This is not impossible. It is only a matter of codifying and universalizing what already exists. There are gaps to be filled. We should have a "Bill of Economic Rights." Then we might properly say: "These are the unsurpassed advantages of citizenship in a democracy. What can be offered in their place by rival totalitarian systems where wealth and freedom alike are destroyed by tyranny and force?" Democracy must set, as its charter for the twentieth century: security without slavery; freedom without poverty; progress without violence. This might be our reply to the so-called "new order," for a reply we must surely make. The totalitarian menace will undoubtedly accelerate the acceptance of such a general political philosophy as is here suggested.

Périgord: Politics

Now, what are the specific and immediate prerequisites of American policy which these Nazi triumphs force upon us and which may so completely alter our traditional way of life? They may be listed as follows: the establishment of an opposing military force, designed to neutralize, if not overwhelm, the systems of the totalitarian states, and to develop the highest national efficiency and discipline; the carrying out of unified governmental planning with thorough discussion and by democratic processes, to strengthen the national economy and mobilize economic resources; the planning of a balanced democratic society, with major attention on social health, the conquest of poverty, the breeding of a better populace, the elimination of controllable pernicious factors in our national life; the development of swift democratic techniques, based upon wide delegation of powers for speedy and efficient action, yet subject to periodic popular control; and the purging from our political life of tenacious local antagonisms and conflicts, and the learning of the art of democratic coöperation.

These, then, much too briefly stated and presented here, of necessity, in synoptic form, are likely to be the main effects of the war upon our political structure and behavior in the United States; but the other American countries are not likely to be thus affected, because their economic organization is not so complex, their political development not so advanced, nor their responsibilities so grave. There is one problem, however, which we all have in common in the Western Hemisphere, and that is the problem of security. The fundamental preoccupation of all Americans is how best to preserve our independence. How is this war going to affect the security of the Western Hemisphere? For, without security, the character of our political life will be substantially altered.

Thus far the safety of the Americas has, in some degree, been assured by our naval and military defenses. But these would have been entirely inadequate to thwart the designs of powerful and ambitious European nations if American security had not been safeguarded by other factors. These are three: distance from aggressive nations, the European balance of power, and British naval strength.

The first and most obvious factor of American security is the distance that separates the Americas from both Europe and Asia. The width of the Atlantic has always prevented any European nation from exerting more than a fraction of its power in our hemisphere, and despite all the progress that has been made in naval construction, the thousands of miles of ocean still contribute greatly to our security. Distance can thus preserve us from serious danger at home; but it cannot preclude all damage. A strong hostile navy could always attempt "hit and run" raids against some of the more exposed parts on our long coastline. Danger from the air, like danger from the sea, could only become really serious if the distance obstacle were materially reduced by the establishment of bases in our hemisphere. Alas, such enemy bases are no longer an impossibility.

It must not be overlooked that our Atlantic barrier narrows in two places to less than 1800 miles, in the north between Ireland and Newfoundland, and in the south between Africa and Brazil. We have taken adequate measures regarding the first, but we have some crucial defensive problems to face with respect to the second.

Périgord: Politics

As to the Pacific, since that ocean is much wider than the Atlantic, it is universally admitted that its protective value is considerably greater. Our West Coast, shielded by the strong and strategically situated Hawaiian base, even if defended by only half of our navy and air force, is entirely out of danger from anything more serious than minor raids.

The second factor in providing security for the Americas has been the European balance of power. The rivalries of Europe have contributed to the safety, welfare, and peaceful growth of the Americas. But if these rivalries are terminated by a German victory that makes Europe a bloc of nations subservient to Berlin, this factor of historic security will disappear. That European bloc, brought under centralized control, would probably seek full access to the vast mineral and agricultural resources of our sparsely populated hemisphere.

The third factor in American security has been the protection afforded by the British navy ever since the Monroe Doctrine was first announced. This British support was not based upon altogether altruistic motives, but rather upon two vital British interests; foreign trade and security of the imperial routes. Of course, the value of this British capacity to protect our hemisphere from Europe depends largely upon the nature of Anglo-American relations. Fortunately, our relationship with Great Britain is basically harmonious, as the many interests which unite us far outweigh our rivalry in world markets. We have consequently a vital national concern in the preservation of Britain's power in the Atlantic.

If Germany wins the war, upon us alone will fall the task of preserving the Monroe Doctrine. A German victory would instantly remove two of the factors of our security: the British navy and the European balance of power. Only the security factor of distance would remain. And this, tapering dangerously in the narrows between Africa and Brazil, would become progressively weaker with increase in the range of action of modern implements of war.

Little wonder, therefore, that we have recently seen a growing interest in Pan-Americanism and hemispheric defense on the part of all the Americas.

Today's deliberate, consistent, and intelligent efforts on the part of the American republics have evolved from an interesting background of trial and error. Strange to say, Pan-Americanism did not originate in the United States, and at first did not find enthusiastic support here. Its "spiritual father" was Simón Bolívar, the George Washington of South America, who liberated from the yoke of Spain the peoples who now make up the republics of Venezuela, Colombia, Ecuador, Peru, and Bolivia. Toward the end of the year 1824, Bolívar, through letters of invitation, called a conference of the Latin American governments, to which the United States was subsequently invited. His instructions to the delegates of Peru, the government of which he then headed, urged them to try to secure a "great compact of union, league, and confederation against Spain and against foreign rule, of whatever character," to negotiate "treaties of friendship, navigation, and commerce with the new American states as allies and confederates," and to obtain the issuance of a proclamation containing "such an energetic and efficient declaration [the Monroe Doctrine] as that made by the President of the United States of America in his message to Congress."

Périgord: Politics 125

That conference met at Panama in 1826. Secretary of State Clay was opposed to the idea of an alliance between the American nations, characterizing such a union as "worse than useless." Two United States delegates were sent, but with very limited powers. One of them died on the way, and the other arrived too late for the meeting. Only a few other nations were represented. A treaty drawn up was never ratified, and the whole affair came to naught. While it is to be regretted that Bolívar's statesmanship was not matched by that of our own government, a beginning had been made.

In 1881, James G. Blaine, Secretary of State under President Garfield, invited the Americas to participate in a conference to be held in Washington the following year "for the purpose of considering and discussing the methods of preventing war between the nations of America." It was hoped that by that date a war then in progress between Chile and Peru would be over. It was not. Moreover, a change in administration occurred, following the assassination of President Garfield, and the invitations were withdrawn. In 1888, in Cleveland's administration, Congress passed a bill authorizing the summoning of such a conference in the following year. In 1889, when Benjamin Harrison had become President and Blaine was again Secretary of State, the first Pan-American Conference assembled at Washington. An arbitration treaty was drafted and signed by eleven nations, but it was never ratified. The most practical result was the establishment of the permanent organization now known as the Pan-American Union. The resolution providing for that Union, first called the Commercial Bureau of the American Republics, was passed on

April 14, the day which has been celebrated every year for half a century as Pan-American Day.

The second Pan-American Conference met at Mexico City in 1901, the third at Rio de Janeiro in 1906, and the fourth at Buenos Aires in 1910. But the fifth Pan-American Conference, scheduled for 1914, was postponed because of the First World War, and was not held until 1923, when it met finally in Santiago, Chile.

Meanwhile, the United States had lost favor with the governments of the other Americas because it had intervened in several Caribbean countries. The Monroe Doctrine, so admired by Simón Bolívar, came to be bitterly criticized by other South American leaders when its spirit was invoked in relation to events in Nicaragua, Haiti, and Santo Domingo. The United States sent troops into Nicaragua in 1912 to protect American lives and property, and kept a "legation guard" detailed there to preserve order until 1930. When civil war in Haiti in 1915 brought danger of European interference, an armed force was sent to that country, which was not withdrawn until 1933. Civil strife caused the same action on our part in Santo Domingo in 1916, where United States troops were stationed until 1924.

These three instances of interference engendered a Latin American distrust of the United States, which was still strong at the sixth Pan-American Conference, held in Havana, Cuba, in 1928. But complete friendliness had been again restored by the time of the seventh Pan-American Conference, at Montevideo, Uruguay, in 1933, and the twenty-one member nations devoted themselves successfully to the task of safeguarding

Périgord: Politics 127

peace among and for the Americas.* The eighth Pan-American Conference was held at Lima, Peru, in 1938.

Under the impact of the present war, Pan-Americanism has entered a completely new phase. Heretofore, our primary Pan-American interest, on the political side, was to maintain peace within the Western Hemisphere rather than guard against danger from abroad. We were concerned chiefly with keeping the American republics from quarreling among themselves, settling through arbitration such quarrels as did arise. Many Latin Americans were, in fact, less worried about a possible attack from Europe than about the danger of aggressive action from the North. Now, with the gradual collapse of collective security in the rest of the world and the increasing dangers to which small and weak nations found themselves exposed, a great change has occurred.

For the first time, a genuine basis for a solid Pan-American front has come into existence. Heretofore, Pan-Americanism had been slow, uphill work. The things that differentiate the twenty-one countries have always been much more marked than any real or fancied similarity. Pan-Americanism has become a reality in the last few months because the one thing that we unquestionably have in common, a desire to retain our independence, now seems so much more important than any or all the things which might tend to divide us.

---

* Important peace instruments negotiated to date by the Pan-American republics have been the Gondra Treaty, sponsored by Manuel Gondra, of Paraguay, in 1923, supplemented, in 1929, by the Inter-American Conciliation Convention and the Inter-American Arbitration Treaty, and the further supplemental Argentine antiwar pact of 1933. These treaties provide peaceable means, so far effective in the Americas, for the settling of international disputes.

Accordingly, soon after the outbreak of the war a meeting of the foreign ministers of the twenty-one republics was summoned. They met in Panama from September 23 to October 3, 1939. With this meeting a new chapter in Pan-Americanism begins. They drew up a Declaration of Neutrality and decided to set up a permanent Neutrality Committee in order to bring their policies into general agreement. They felt at that time that a declaration of neutrality would be a guaranty of security. But as the war progressed, neutrality revealed itself to be very poor protection indeed. Neutral, as well as belligerent, nations were overrun and conquered. Denmark, Norway, Holland, Belgium fell before the German onslaught. This tremendous upheaval in the international situation brought with it a host of problems. A new consultation of American ministers became imperative.

The meeting was convoked at Havana, July 21, 1940. It was the hope of President Roosevelt that the American nations would send their ministers of foreign affairs or secretaries of state. Only eleven did so. The others gave various excuses—or were they welcome pretexts?—such as the great distances to Cuba, the pressure of business at home, the critical state of international problems. All the nations, however, sent delegates of ability and distinction. There were in all 135 delegates, including aides or legal advisers. As I was fortunate enough to be in attendance, I shall take the liberty of sharing with you a few personal impressions.

The American delegation was headed by Secretary of State Cordell Hull. He was everywhere greeted with evidences of respect and affection. As he walked up the long flight of steps

Périgord: Politics

which led into the beautiful white marble building that is the Cuban capitol, the guard of honor presented arms and the bands played the "Star Spangled Banner." When he entered the beautifully decorated chamber of the House of Representatives, all the delegates arose, and the applause was spontaneous, sincere, and prolonged. As he went to the section reserved for the American delegation, many of the most prominent delegates, who evidently had worked with him at previous conferences, walked over to him and extended greetings. Amidst the general enthusiasm, across the semicircle one delegation appeared reserved and unmoved: it was the delegation from Argentina, the ever vigilant critic and rival leader. Its head, a venerable, dignified, scholarly-looking statesman, Leopoldo Melo, remained grave and aloof. Secretary Hull grasped the meaning of the situation instantly. With great deference he left his desk, walked over to the Argentinian delegation, and offered his hand to Leopoldo Melo. Señor Melo smiled, evidently pleased and relieved. Compliments were exchanged. All the delegates understood. The large hall rang with applause, and that gracious gesture subsequently helped greatly to remove misgivings and promote closer cooperation. Cordell Hull, blending unfailing Southern courtesy and American firmness, is entitled to much of the credit for the success of the Havana Conference.

I wish I had the time to describe to you the many eloquent, forceful addresses, brilliant in content and form, delivered by the leading delegates. I am sure that your regard for the intelligence, distinction, general culture, legal knowledge of the Latin Americans would be materially increased. Of course the one address most eagerly awaited was that of Cordell Hull. He knew he was speaking to a critical audience, in defense of a program facing discouraging obstacles. He spoke with great force, at times with deep emotion, but with great tact, avoiding even the semblance of dictation.

> We are here [he began] as representatives of the twenty-one free and independent American republics. We meet when world conditions are perhaps graver than they have ever been before. Our purpose is to devise concrete measures by which a number of pressing problems may be met. Our objective is to safeguard the independence, the peace, and the well-being of the American republics....
> It has been increasingly clear that our nations must not blind themselves into fatal complacency, as so many nations have done to their mortal sorrow, regarding the possibility of attack against them from without or of externally directed attempts from within to undermine their national strength and to subvert their cherished social and political institutions, or both.
> Too many nations have only recently paid a tragic price for confidently placing reliance for their safety and security solely upon clearly expressed desires to remain at peace, upon unequivocally proclaimed neutrality, upon scrupulous avoidance of provocation. Conquerors, invaders, and destroyers ignore or brush aside reasons such as these.

One of the more noticeably applauded parts of his address was that devoted to explaining the difference between our Monroe Doctrine and the counterfeit "Monroe Doctrine" enunciated by Germany, Italy, and Japan, which "instead of resting on the respect for existing sovereignties, is only a pretext for military conquest and complete economic and political domination by certain powers of other free and independent peoples."

Périgord: Politics

In a warmly applauded and indeed felicitous summary of America's fundamental political philosophy, Secretary Hull declared:

> Mankind can advance only when human freedom is secure; when the right of self-government is safeguarded; when all nations recognize each other's right to conduct its internal affairs free from outside interference; when there exists among nations respect for the pledged word, determination to abstain from the use of armed force in pursuit of policy, and willingness to settle controversies by none but peaceful means; when international economic relations are based upon mutual benefit, equality of treatment, and fair dealing.

In conclusion he issued a stern warning, saying that while we entertain no enmity toward anyone, we are becoming increasingly aware of dangers about us and we have resolved to take adequate measures for our protection. At the various plenary sessions nearly every speaker reëchoed these declarations.

The delegates at Havana were confronted with three sets of problems and conditions. The first related to the transfer of sovereignty over certain islands and regions from one North American state to another. The second involved the threat of subversive activities in American nations, directed from outside the continent. The third comprised extremely grave economic difficulties and dislocations resulting from the war.

The third of these problems has been ably discussed in the previous lectures of this series. As the second problem, that relating to fifth-column activities, was neither thoroughly nor vigorously dealt with, we shall concentrate on the first, which is of the utmost political gravity, namely, the transfer of territories held by European powers.

In the eyes of American statesmen, two very definite dangers have been created as a result of the rapid developments in Europe. Germany might demand outright control of the American colonies belonging to the European countries she had overrun: at this date, Denmark, The Netherlands, France. Or, Germany might permit the defeated powers to retain their American colonies while indirectly controlling them through puppet governments. Obviously, the United States could not remain indifferent to either direct or indirect control by Germany of possessions so closely connected with its security. So, on June 18, the day after the fall of France, the State Department had addressed a note to Germany and Italy declaring that the United States would not recognize any transfer and would not acquiesce in any attempt to transfer any geographic region of the Western Hemisphere from one non-American power to another non-American power. Both Houses of Congress had adopted similar resolutions.

This declaration was made because of the urgency of the situation, but such one-sided action would scarcely have harmonized with the Pan-American policy we have so carefully fostered during recent years. This policy calls for consultations of all the American nations whenever an important issue arises affecting their common welfare.

It was gratifying to see at Havana how Latin American interests for once seemed to be nearly identical with our own. This was at last a rare opportunity to emphasize American solidarity. For many Latin Americans, the Monroe Doctrine

Périgord: Politics 133

had unpleasant associations. Since the Doctrine itself was none too popular with Latin Americans, why not supplement it with a common statement of policy to which all Americans could agree? Or, as it has been expressed, why not "continentalize" the Monroe Doctrine? Essentially, this was the outstanding achievement of the Havana Conference, and it may prove one of the most important dates in the history of Pan-Americanism.

The resolutions adopted state a straightforward and realistic policy. They declare that all twenty-one American republics "would consider any transfer or attempt to transfer sovereignty" of American soil from one European power to another "as contrary to American sentiments, principles, and rights of American states to maintain their security and political independence." In these words our neighbors in the Western world deliberately approve our own long-standing interpretation of the Monroe Doctrine on the "transfer" question.

In order to give effect to this declaration, an "emergency committee" was created, whose duties are to administer temporarily the affairs of any area "in danger of becoming the subject-matter of exchange of territories or sovereignty." It was further provided that "should the need for emergency action be so urgent that action of the committee cannot be awaited, any of the American republics, individually or jointly with others, shall have the right to act in a manner which its own defense or that of the continent requires"—referring its action to the committee later. In other words, should the United States itself interfere alone or in collaboration with another state, in any attempted transfer of colonies or islands, it would be acting not only in its own name, but in the name of all the American republics.

Nazi and Fascist newspapers, during the Havana Conference, realized the importance of the proceedings and did their utmost to create friction and distrust. Their favorite stratagem was to play up Argentina's apparent unwillingness to coöperate and her tendency to adopt a position opposed to that of the United States. This is neither entirely accurate nor fair to Argentina. It is true that Argentina has been closer to Europe than has any other American state. Most of her trade has traditionally been with Great Britain; intellectually she has been very close to France. She is distant from the United States both geographically and culturally. Moreover, Argentina is proud of her position as the most advanced of the Latin American countries and considers herself their natural leader. Such being the case, Argentina has tended to maintain an independent attitude at Pan-American gatherings. Actually, Argentina's policy at Havana, an attitude of hesitation and caution, was not by any means illogical. She had little interest in the Caribbean islands. She was interested in the Falkland Islands, but, as one may readily surmise, this was not up for discussion. Argentina pointed out that an attempt to take over the Caribbean colonies might, if resisted, amount to an act of war. Would the American republics be willing to face this possibility? Furthermore, if an angry European power should attempt reprisals, who would guarantee Argentina's defense? Distant as she is from our shores, Argentina is not certain that the United States either could or would defend her.

Périgord: Politics

After the adjournment of the Havana Conference on July 30, important developments took place which bore closely upon the matter under discussion. On September 3, President Roosevelt announced that the United States government had secured 99-year leases for naval and air bases on eight British possessions. Our new defense line thus extends 4500 miles from Newfoundland in the north to British Guiana in the south. The possession of these bases completes our control of the Caribbean.

This transaction did not, of course, fall within the terms of the Havana agreement, for no actual transfer of sovereignty was involved. Nevertheless, it has greatly increased the ability of the United States to defend itself and to defend the hemisphere, and began to provide an answer to the anxious question of Latin Americans, What can you do for us if we side with you?

This study would be sadly incomplete if no mention were made of the Dominion of Canada, which plays so brave and vital a part in the present conflict. Her political, economic, and social life has been affected more deeply than that of any other American nation, as she is actually at war with Germany. An agreement of the greatest importance between Canada and the United States was reached on August 17, 1940; it established a permanent Joint Board on Defense. This action has a significant bearing upon our Pan-American policy, first, because the Joint Board will serve as a model for other two-party boards through which the United States and Latin American countries might coöperate; secondly, because it raises the possibility of closer Canadian coöperation with the Pan-American group.

Canada occupies a curious dual position. Geographically she is an important segment of the Western Hemisphere. Politically she is a member of the British Commonwealth of Nations. As a result of her political ties with Europe, the Dominion is not an official member of the Pan-American family of nations. She is not a member of the Pan-American Union and does not have delegates at the Pan-American conferences. Unofficially, however, she has observers present at those meetings.

There is a small but important group in Canada which would like to see a strengthening of the Dominion's ties with the rest of the continent. Last August, Professor Frank Underhill of Toronto University told the Canadian Institute of Economics and Politics, "We have now two loyalties, one to Britain, the other to North America. I venture to say the second, North America, is going to be supreme now."

Improvement of Canadian-American relations has proceeded rapidly. The conclusion of a Canadian-American reciprocal trade agreement in 1935, its renewal and extension three years later, President Roosevelt's visits to Canada and his pledge, in 1938, that her territorial integrity would be preserved against aggression, and the closer military and economic coöperation in mutual defense are milestones in the swift progress toward an understanding to which it is difficult to set a limit. For if the British Isles were to fall, Canada would find comfort as well as security in an entirely new political association.

The announcement of the defense agreement between the United States and Canada, and the deal with Great Britain

Périgord: Politics 137

for exchanging destroyers and bases, have stirred conflicting emotions in Latin America. Most Latin American commentators agree that the United States is now in a better position to undertake both its own defense and that of the hemisphere. There is a tendency, however, particularly in the Argentine press, to inquire whether the United States were not being brought perilously near to actual belligerency by these bold moves. Moreover, some of the Latin American countries may have resented the fact that we proceeded so soon after the Havana Conference to act on our own initiative. If so, they must have been comforted by the announcement of Secretary Hull on September 7, 1940, that the Latin American states are welcome to the use of the newly acquired bases.

This rapid survey would appear too optimistic if we failed to take into account some of the stern realities of the American drama. If the impact of the war has produced less than an impregnable and unanimous military, economic, and political front against the totalitarian states, this relative failure cannot be imputed to American statesmen. It is due primarily to the natural conflicts of interests of the American nations and to the realities which a Good Neighbor policy cannot efface.

In the first place, the Western Hemisphere is not, as so many people assume, a military, economic, and political unit. It is composed of nations as different in racial origins, social forms, military strength, economic independence, and political thought as those which make up Europe.

In the second place, our primary objective is quite naturally the defense of the continental United States and of its social and political system, an objective not equally dear and vital to all American nations. Nor are all their governments convinced that our system, particularly if Germany defeats Great Britain, affords the best protection of their interests. They have surpluses in competition with our own; their rulers are not democratic in spirit; they doubt the ability or willingness of succeeding United States administrations to support their economy and to give them military protection.

In the third place, some of the Latin American nations, while willing to accept loans from the United States, are deeply influenced by German and Italian residents whose leadership their upper classes prefer to that of the United States.

The story of the war thus far makes it clear beyond doubt that unless the Latin American nations act in full military, economic, and political accord with the United States, not one is strong enough to resist capture by the conquerors of Europe. Is such concert obtainable, and if not, can we protect them?

This war presents the greatest opportunity the United States has had for Western Hemisphere unity and also raises one of the most trying problems. The majority of people in Latin America are aroused and concerned over German aggressions; they feel more friendly toward the United States than ever before. But simultaneously, vigorous minority groups in every country, many of them already controlled by Hitler, are doing their utmost to sabotage Western Hemisphere harmony.

What we frequently overlook when speaking of Latin America is that most of its republics never have been actual democracies. They are a collection of oligarchies in which the aristocratic families, many of them descended from the Spanish conquistadores and since grown affluent on copper, tin, meat, and coffee, have completely dominated their countries. The countries of Latin America have long known the dictator, the coup d'état, the political revolution. Their soil is, for many reasons, suited to the growth of the totalitarian state. The advent of Hitler, therefore, does not particularly disturb them except so far as he is likely to upset their system of land and mineral ownership with a new National Socialism. They may not fight enthusiastically for our type of democracy, but they will fight for their independence, and in that contingency they stand desperately in need of our help.

This task of defending the hemisphere would be far from easy, because most of South America is a liability, not an asset, in our strategic position. While its wealth and resources exert a strong magnetic attraction on Europe and Asia, its own defensive capacity is exceedingly weak. All the nations of South America lack the industrial development and the political, economic, and social maturity which give the powers of Europe such capacity for war. This means that the real burden of defending South America must fall upon us, with only limited assistance from our sister republics beyond Panama.

In South America the danger point is Brazil, once the object of special attention by the German emperor, and now bulking large in the eyes of the Hitler regime. Brazil, because it juts so far toward the Eastern Hemisphere, is the strategic key to the Atlantic defense of South America. And, at the same time, it is a vital actual and potential source of the essential raw materials the United States requires. Geography, climate, and the racial texture of its people make Brazil a prospective hunting ground for the Nazi empire builders. Should Great Britain be defeated, our Brazilian supply base and defensive bastion will be exposed to direct attack, and with it the whole of South America.

The war is fostering a certain psychological unity which should be translated without delay into something more tangible. We must provide a coördination of all constructive currents and the elimination of all destructive ones. It will be best if the initial steps toward unification are taken in the economic field, in which all nations, large as well as small, may find an easily grasped advantage. The first step might be a customs union, eliminating artificial barriers to commerce. The second should be the introduction of a common monetary unit.

The delegates at the Havana Conference believed, and wisely so, that the political solidarity of the hemisphere will depend largely upon the effectiveness of economic coöperation, and proposed the following measures as likely to give the best results: (1) encouragement of the production of rubber and tin; (2) purchase in Latin America of the numerous other products which the United States now buys elsewhere; (3) provision of capital for the development of new industries; (4) establishment of a Latin American bank; (5) improvement of transportation facilities; (6) raising of the standard of life; (7) encouragement of Latin American trade. This is a truly constructive policy, which would provide the most effective answer to German intrigue.

Périgord: Politics

It is clear that Hitler wishes to monopolize the extensive unexploited natural resources and markets of South America, and that he is ready to reach toward that goal by setting up governments pledged to coöperation with the Axis. Nazi propaganda, taking advantage of every possible difference between the United States and Latin America, between one country and another in South America, and between groups and classes in each nation, aims at breaking down national unity and hemispheric coöperation; it seeks to create chaos and confusion and to prepare the way for fifth columnists to strike deliberately weakened peoples and governments when the time comes.

Many South American countries are afraid that Germany will win, that she will make good her threats to force them into economic subjugation, and that the United States will be neither willing nor able to do anything about it. It is not too late for us to offset the Nazi drive if we act promptly and decisively—if we show the Latin Americans that we take a realistic attitude toward our responsibility for world leadership forced upon us by the European war, that we will stand for no more fifth-column nonsense in the Western Hemisphere, and that we have both the will and the power to protect our friends and put teeth into the Monroe Doctrine. The problem is to save the South American countries from being compelled by the hard facts of self-preservation to become economic colonies of Germany.

We must meet fire with fire—fight anti-American propaganda with anti-Nazi propaganda. We must have complete military coördination of all available forces for the defense of the Western Hemisphere. We must have naval and air bases wherever needed. We must have naval, military, and aviation missions in the countries vital to hemispheric defense. We must have a sufficient number of long-range bombers to oppose a powerful striking force to any invading fleet. It is gratifying to see that during the last few months definite results have been attained and that nearly all countries, Mexico in the lead, have shown an unexpected spirit of coöperation.

While it is clear that the Americas will not and cannot renounce their diversity, always a source of charm and genius, they must coördinate and discipline their diversity, in order to guarantee their survival. Our primary task is to assist them with all the tact possible in this delicate undertaking.

In this rapid and incomplete review of the political situation of the Americas, I have endeavored to outline our immediate duties. Indeed, they are not all of our choosing. Many are forced upon us by world conditions and we cannot ignore them. They are not, however, our final goal. Our highest ambition is to be of assistance, with our sense of justice even more than with our strength, in the organization of a worldwide commonwealth of nations based upon international fair play and coöperation.

This is yet the greatest challenge which has come to our nation. Shall we be equal to our task? There is joy and comfort in the thought that all of us can help to provide the answer.

THE WAR AND CULTURAL RELATIONS

CÉSAR BARJA
PROFESSOR OF SPANISH
IN THE UNIVERSITY OF CALIFORNIA

Lecture delivered May 6, 1941

THE WAR AND CULTURAL RELATIONS

THE GENERAL relationship between America and Europe, ever an interesting subject since the days of the discovery of the New World, has assumed a very special character during the last forty years or so. Briefly, what has happened during these years is that the old traditional relationship, in which Europe led, has gradually been changing to one in which America appears more and more as the leader, and Europe as more and more dependent on America. Especially since the fateful years 1914–1918 this process has been going on so rapidly and so violently as to have totally upset the old order of things. Today the situation is perfectly evident: for all practical purposes, the American continent has displaced Europe from its position as the dominant force. Or, to be more specific, the United States has displaced Europe, the rest of the American continent being left, with respect to the United States, in a position not very dissimilar to that of Europe itself. Neither London, nor Paris, nor Berlin, nor, for that matter, Buenos Aires, but rather Washington is today the political and economic center of gravity of the Old and the New Worlds, which is the same as to say of the whole world.

If we now ask ourselves what have been the causes that have brought about this displacement of Europe by America, two sets of factors present themselves for consideration, one having to do with the American, the other with the European, side of the question.

As to the factors relating to the American side, they are so plain and so self-evident that to enunciate them is to understand them. With a new continent much bigger and much richer than Europe, both in the absolute sense and in proportion to the number of people it has to support; with a continent politically organized, especially as far as the United States is concerned, on a basis particularly well adapted to the economic development of its enormous resources, America's growth in power belongs simply to the order of historical fatalities. This growth, under abnormal circumstances, might have been retarded, as it sometimes has been, especially in Latin America, but it could never have been prevented. Europe knew this a long time ago; one may say that it knew it even before the modern European man had set foot on the American continent. It was on his third trip that Columbus, half lost in the Gulf of Paria, faced for the first time the coast of the American mainland. Charmed by what he had before his eyes, he fell into one of his usual mystic-Biblical raptures. This time he was convinced, or half-convinced, that what lay in front of him was nothing less than the Earthly Paradise itself, to the identification of which he thought it proper to devote some very entertaining considerations. The geographical identification was, of course, slightly erroneous, but great men are seldom entirely wrong, and this vision, or rather this intuition, of Columbus was, as far as the potentialities of America are concerned, fundamentally right.

But while this natural growth of America was a most influential factor in the upsetting of the balance of power between the Old and the New Worlds, it is doubtful whether its effects would have been so immediate and so noticeable had it not been for the fact that just as America was coming up, Europe was going down. It was not only that America was moving forward; it was also that Europe was moving backward. Of this double movement, like two trains running in opposite directions, the enormous disproportion in power of the two continents appears today as the net result. Hence the impossibility of separating the American from the European side of the question.

Unfortunately, however, plain and self-evident as we see the American side of the question to be, the European side is so confused and so problematic that one hardly knows where to begin to look at it. Here the threads of a multiple variety of aspects cross and recross in the most inextricable tangle, so that one is never sure whether what he has before his eyes is a beginning or an end, a cause or an effect.

For our purpose here one single observation will suffice, and that is the recognition of the fact, for a fact undoubtedly it is, that the troubles of Europe are as much of an external as of an internal nature, that they are material as well as spiritual. It is just this that makes the situation infinitely more complex. We must not forget that this is not, after all, the first time that Europe has gone through a crisis, nor is war over there to be considered as a new experience. The truth is rather that crises and troubles of one kind or another, and wars fought for this or the other purpose or for no purpose at all, have been such frequent occurrences in the history of the Old World as to constitute an almost normal situation. European culture is not the artificial flower of any peaceloving Arcadia; even more than with love, it has been fertilized with blood. Yet the fact remains that after each of these many social and political convulsions Europe has always been capable of pulling itself together and once more resuming its march forward. This time, however, the situation appears to be an entirely different one. Since the tragic holocaust of 1914–1918, Europe has not been able to recover. It may be argued, of course, that the War of 1914–1918 was on a much larger scale, was infinitely more devastating and more demoralizing than any previous war.

Still, other factors might be mentioned, among them being the fact, by no means insignificant, of the ever-increasing economic competition that Europe has had to face as a consequence of the likewise ever-increasing industrial and commercial expansion of America. But real and important as the economic factor undoubtedly has been, it would be wrong to conclude that all of Europe's troubles are only of an economic nature, or due only to economic causes. The economic situation itself was during all these years a changeable one, now better, now worse, while the troubles followed the line of a continual crescendo. Furthermore, phenomena like the militant, aggressive nationalism that set country against country—a reality long before 1914—and the social-political convulsions out of which the present dictatorial regimes grew, to say nothing of the general condition of hatred and violence that dominated public and private relations, far transcend any purely economic interpretation, whatever their original economic import may have been. It is noteworthy in this connection that, evident as the troubles were, no real effort was made, nor did the desire seem to exist on anyone's part, to change a situation which no one liked and which everyone was convinced would sooner or later lead to the present catastrophe. By this I do not mean the passive desire to see things change by themselves, but the active desire to look at a situation squarely and be ready to make the necessary sacrifices to change it. This is, it seems to me, highly significant, and would by itself serve as proof that, however bad the material conditions of life may have been, the troubles from which Europe suffers are much deeper and due to much deeper causes than mere economic distress.

But the strongest corroboration of this point is to be found in the fact that not only were the troubles not confined to the sphere of material interests; a condition of disorder and confusion not unlike that prevailing in the political, economic, and social aspects of life existed also in the more intimate order of the intellectual and spiritual culture of the Continent.

This is not the occasion, of course, to enter into a detailed discussion of the whole panorama of European culture, as this panorama has been unfolding since, let us say, the beginning of the present century. One or two considerations, however, may be permissible here.

To say that Europe has not had during these last forty years an active cultural life would by no means be correct. Even leaving aside the more specialized fields of science and scientific research, a very active movement has been going on in philosophy, literature, and art, fields in which, better than in any other, the ideological and spiritual orientation of a culture as a human and social event reveals itself at a given moment. Neither would it be correct to say that no important single works have been produced in these as well as in other fields of culture. Both the quantity of this cultural activity and the quality of some or even all of its products are, however, elements of secondary importance. What is of primary importance is the absence in all this vast cultural activity and production of that sense of direction which results from the existence of a clear, well-defined set of ideas or principles the validity of which is implicitly accepted, if not as fixed rule, at least as a line of orientation. Whenever such a set of clear, well-defined ideas or principles is lacking, there can be neither a sense of the values to be realized nor the spirit of discipline necessary to realize them, so that, however important in other respects a cultural movement may be, it must remain a blind enterprise, like a collection of more or less accidental events. A culture is not a series of paths running in the most unexpected and capricious directions. It is, above all, if it is to be anything worthy of the name, a main road and a line of direction, regardless of how numerous and varied the byways may then be. A culture is, in short, an *order* of things, not a disorder; its essence is one of clarification, not one of confusion. A main road and a line of direction, an order, however, is exactly what European culture has not been for a long time and what it is not today; so much so, that, limiting ourselves to the indicated fields of philosophy, literature, and art, and affirming once more that important works have been produced in each and all of these fields, it would at least be questionable whether, in the sense just explained, Europe has had during all these last forty years any real philosophic, literary, and artistic culture, that is to say, a basic philosophic, literary, and artistic conception, something which in the final analysis comes to be a conception of life and culture themselves. That there should have been so many, so strange, and so heterogenous philosophic, literary, and artistic experiments and novelties is perhaps in itself the best proof that no such basic conception existed.

Curiously, the strongest bond uniting all or most of the various cultural manifestations in each and all of these fields has been one of a rather negative nature, namely, the desire to break with the past and react against it. Thus, more than as an action, this cultural movement appears as a reaction; rather than forward, it has been looking backward, not because it loved the past, but because it hated it and wished to break with it. This break between past and present has been the dominant feature of contemporary European culture, as it has also been the dominant feature of the contemporary European mind and soul.

Were this the occasion for it, it would be interesting to try now to find out what the meaning of so abrupt and so violent a breaking-off with the past may be. Perhaps it would then be seen that what happened was that the European man in general, and the European intellectual in particular, lost faith in most of the traditional values, and, above all, in that value which for hundreds of years had been the foundation of most of the others, that is to say, the value of reason itself, either because reason can no longer be trusted as a means of knowledge, as is asserted by some, or because it cannot be trusted as a norm of conduct, as is protested by others. Hence, of course, the consequent glorification, in philosophy as well as in psychology, in literature as well as in art, of the intuitional and vitalistic elements, the unconscious and the subconscious, and, in short, of all the semimystic and more or less irrational instincts and impulses of the spontaneous, animal life. Names as illustrious as those of Bergson in philosophy, Freud in psychology, and D. H. Lawrence in literature speak for themselves in this connection. Should we be surprised, then, that exactly the same antirational tendency should have found expression in the social and political life of the continent? The truth is, rather, that Hitler's emotionalism and his mystic sense of destiny are also an essential part of the present panorama of European culture.

But I must interrupt these considerations here. It was my purpose only to show that, disorderly and confused as the external, material life of Europe has been, its internal, intellectual and spiritual life has been equally so; or, to put it in words that will convey an idea of what I believe to be at the bottom of the whole situation, a basic demoralization has dominated contemporary European life in the political, social, and economic spheres, and in intellectual and spiritual matters as well. This demoralization, in itself the consequence of the disintegration of all faith in the traditional, basic values of life and culture, I consider to be the fundamental trouble in the European situation. To take an outstanding example, it was neither Stalin, nor Mussolini, nor Hitler that killed the democratic ideal of government in Europe. If it is true that half of the battles that are won are only the battles that the enemy loses, then it may properly be said that the battle won

Barja: Culture

by these three gentlemen was only the battle lost by the so-called democracies of Europe, the reason being that the ideal of democracy was already dead in the minds and hearts of the people of these democracies.

It is perhaps not an accident that the most typical form of philosophic speculation during all these years should have turned round the so-called philosophy of values, as represented by men like Münsterberg, Rickert, Max Scheler, and so forth. One always speculates about the things one does not possess. Now, translated in plain, human terms, the significance of this philosophy is very simple. It means: all traditional values being in a condition of bankruptcy, let us see how to build new ones to put in their place, or let us see, at least, how to rehabilitate the old ones—a noble effort, the only fault of which is to forget that values, old or new, do not support themselves but must be supported by a faith in them. This faith gone, all is gone. On nothing, nothing can be built. Even the weathervane, though it is meant only to keep turning round, must rest on some fixed point. Such a fixed point, however, is what European, perhaps all Western life and culture, lack. Hence the demoralization referred to.

Needless to say, the result of all this, as far as the reaction outside Europe is concerned, was just what might have been expected. Expressed in financial terms, European stock has for years now been selling below par, which is tantamount to saying that Europe has been losing prestige and authority in the eyes of the world, and very much so in the eyes of Americans. This is precisely what the distinguished European delegates who in 1936 attended the Seventh Conversation of the Institute of Intellectual Coöperation of the League of Nations held in Buenos Aires were plainly told by several of the no less distinguished American delegates. As expressed by one of them, the Argentinian Señor Juan B. Terán, "A revolutionary phenomenon has taken place in the cultural relations between Europe and America during the present century. There has been a divorce, a repudiation. Europe has lost in the eyes of the Sixth Continent the prestige it once had of being an almost sacred model. The Great War, the subsequent revolutions, and the Spanish Civil War have been a death blow to our faith in European culture."[1] It was not only, therefore, that America displaced Europe; it was that culturally and ethically Europe displaced itself. This is the naked truth of the matter, a truth of which, even more than the other peoples, Europeans themselves have been conscious.

So far I have been referring to the displacement of Europe by America in rather general terms. A word of explanation will now be in order.

As things stand at present, such a displacement is an accomplished fact in the fields of economics and finance as well as in the realm of international politics. No doubt, I imagine, can exist on this point. In the order of cultural things, however, matters stand differently, and it would be impossible to say that Europe has been displaced from its continental leadership either by America or by any other nation or continent. This is to deny neither the reality of the tremendous cultural progress made by America nor the disorderly and confused condition in which we have said European culture

---

[1] *Europa: America Latina* (Buenos Aires, 1937), p. 239.

Barja: Culture 155

has been for many years. It is simply to recognize the fact that a culture is not a thing that can be improvised in so short a time of settled, nationally and spiritually integrated life as America has had. This is especially true of those aspects of culture which, because of their essential dependence on the personal, subjective element of the human spirit of which they are the autonomous creation as well as the autonomous expression, can only develop along the lines of the slow process followed by the development of the human spirit itself. The case of the United States, by far the most advanced country of the whole American continent, offers us a typical example of this in the disproportion between the almost absolute independence of its scientific and technological culture, on the one hand, and the much more relative independence of its literary and artistic culture, on the other. And what is true of the United States is still more true of Latin America, where scientific and technological culture is much less advanced.

With these considerations in mind, let us come to the concrete question of the meaning of the war to the Americas from the cultural viewpoint. What can this meaning be?

While other effects of the war are more or less problematic, there is one the reality of which is already before us, and that is the dislocation of the cultural relations between the Old and the New Worlds. As a matter of fact, in one aspect at least, this dislocation had already begun before September, 1939. I am thinking in this connection of the, in truth, unique spectacle of hundreds of European intellectuals who, because of the conditions prevailing on the other side of the Atlantic, have been forced to emigrate to America. The exodus may not yet be over, for should Germany win the war, and should the American countries be willing to receive them, it is certain that many more would be coming.

As we all know, some of the most distinguished names of present-day European scientific, philosophic, literary, and artistic culture are included among those of the exiles now living and working in both North and South America. Aside from all humanitarian considerations, and the unavoidable inconveniences resulting from the absorption in so short a time of so large a number of intellectual workers, I do not see how their presence on this side of the Atlantic could be anything but a gain, and a most important gain indeed, to the cultural life of the Americas.

The dislocation of which I am now thinking is, however, not only of a different, but of an opposite, nature. For while this coming to America of hundreds of European intellectuals will serve, temporarily at least, to establish closer cultural relations between European and American minds, the result of the dislocation brought about by the war is that these relations have already been reduced to a minimum, and bid fair to become practically nonexistent. This is the immediate effect of the war. It is also, as I see it, the main factor to be borne in mind when thinking of the meaning of the war for the Americas from the cultural viewpoint. Not because such an effect was unexpected—far from it,—but because it is the beginning of a situation which, regardless of how long the war may last and of how it may end, is bound to be with us for a very long time to come.

It is, of course, a purely speculative matter to try to figure out what postwar Europe will look like. That a long period of reconstruction will follow, assuming that enough strength is left for it, is, I suppose, a most natural assumption. What is not at all clear is when this work of reconstruction will really begin and along what lines it will be conducted. The end of the war itself, understanding by the war the conflict now in progress between Germany and England, may or may not mean anything in this connection. Maybe this is the last act of a gruesome tragedy; maybe it is but the first act of a drama the nature and extension of which will be revealed only as it develops. We must not forget that just as continental Europe was divided vertically by the hates of a resentful, aggressive nationalism, so was it also divided horizontally by the hates of a still more resentful and more aggressive opposition of class ideologies and interests. The political aspect of the struggle has thus far obscured the social implications of the problem, though the war itself is assuming more and more a political-social-economic significance. Perhaps a long period of social convulsions and dislocations will be the aftermath of the war. Were this to happen, not only would the reconstruction of Europe be greatly delayed, but the very type of European culture, especially in its social aspects, would be radically changed.

Be this as it may, the one thing certain is, I repeat, that a long time will have to pass before European culture recovers sufficiently to become again an influential factor. It is no easy task, even under the most favorable circumstances, to rehabilitate the cultural life of a country, much less of a whole continent, as deeply and as thoroughly disorganized as Europe is today. And to this must then be added the internal condition of European culture itself as pictured a moment ago. Even if this culture is not so decadent and so fatally doomed as Spengler emphatically affirms and Professor Arnold J. Toynbee cautiously suggests, it certainly is not in a healthy condition. This internal recovery of European culture, still more than the external recovery of the continent, is no less surely bound to be a very slow and very long process.

It is, then, this practical suspension of cultural relations between the Old and the New Worlds that we are confronted with. What will be the consequence of this, as far as American culture is concerned?

If an answer can be given in a few direct and simple words to a question like this, which carries along with it a whole series of implications, then I should say that the consequence will be to stimulate and accelerate the affirmation and definition of American culture as more independent and self-sufficient than has been the case so far. The process may be called one of the Americanization of American culture, for that is, in reality, what it will amount to, and as such it will be the natural complement to American political and economic independence. If American culture has until now, as to a noticeable degree it undoubtedly has, looked rather toward the outside across the Atlantic, from now on it will naturally look more toward the inside, within itself, its future growth thus becoming less external and more internal, less mechanic and more organic, or, if I may say so, less colonial and more national or even continental. Mention is to be made also of another cause that will contribute no less to the same

Barja: Culture 159

result, and that is the general intensification of nationalistic feeling in the countries of this hemisphere, a phenomenon the reality of which, as an immediate result of the war, is already perfectly evident.

Whether this acceleration of a process which, under normal circumstances, would have been accomplished along the lines of a regular, slower evolution, will or will not be detrimental to the cause of American culture, is of course something that time alone will tell. As far as I can see, the situation seems to be one of those in which the advantages and the disadvantages will end by compensating each other, with the possibility, and even the probability, that the advantages will finally well exceed the disadvantages. At the stage at which American culture has already arrived, there seems to be no reason why it should not be able to continue a development of its own. As it is, perhaps American culture as a whole suffers right now from a little too much subordination to European models, and what it needs is precisely to free itself from much of this foreign influence. As a matter of fact, this is what has already been happening for a number of years, in the United States in particular, and the results, as far as I can see, have been most satisfactory in the field of scientific work as well as in literature and, in part, also in art. Traditions undoubtedly count for much in matters of culture, but so also does freedom of expression.

Assuming, then, that such will be the meaning of the war to the Americas from the cultural viewpoint, it may now be asked along what lines this affirmation and definition of American culture is most likely to take place. Will American culture, once freed from the influence of Europe, still remain more or less a prolongation of European culture, or will it perchance develop into a new type?

European culture and American culture are today, to all intents and purposes, one and the same. They are the two main branches of what is generally called Western culture. An essential solidarity, resulting from the basic conceptions of the individual and society, science and art, philosophy, literature, religion, and so on, exists between these two branches, such conceptions being in themselves, for the most part, the legacy inherited by modern Europe from the Graeco-Roman and the medieval-Christian traditions, and by America through the intermediary of modern Europe. To suppose that American culture, once freed from the influence of Europe, could develop along any other lines than those of Western culture, would, therefore, be simply unthinkable. This, however, is only one aspect of the question, for as unthinkable as the foregoing supposition would be, it would be equally unthinkable to imagine that, as it goes on affirming itself as more and more independent, American culture will remain a mere prolongation of European culture. Just as a culture cannot be improvised, neither can it be prevented from developing new traits and peculiarities. I am speaking, of course, of a culture which, as in the case under consideration, is alive and, consequently, in process of growth. Every culture, in the last analysis, tastes of the soil upon which it has grown. Even when the main lines of future development are, as they are in the present case, more or less drawn up beforehand, the lines themselves are winding and elastic enough to permit

Barja: Culture

of very many and very substantial deviations. It was, after all, within the same main lines of Western culture that the varied mosaic of present European cultures, each marked with the traits of a certain national, spiritual personality, grew up. What we call European culture, or, for that matter, Western culture, is only the common denominator of a series of otherwise very different national cultures. We all know that.

But so do we know also that, already today, if it is impossible to say that American culture, in its present form, is essentially different from that of Europe, it is equally impossible to say that it is exactly identical. The truth of the matter is that present-day American culture also, whether taken as a whole or in each of its single national manifestations, presents itself already as an additional series of variations of that common denominator which we said Western culture was. As such it has its peculiar characteristics, reflects a certain mental and psychological disposition, makes use of its special methods, and moves according to a rhythm and a tempo of its own. In short, it is the revelation of a spirit which, not yet fully developed and probably handicapped in its free expression by the pressure of too much foreign influence, appears as already different from anything European.

Now, it seems to me only natural that as the process of the affirmation and definition of American culture goes on, not only will the present differences between it and European culture be retained, but new and more signficant ones are most likely to develop, with the result that American culture will diverge more and more from the European, perhaps also from the Western model, as this model is known to us today.

There are a number of considerations that lead me to believe that this will, in fact, occur: namely, the racial composition of America, mixing up into one single enormous North American bowl and one single enormous South American bowl the racial spirit which in Europe has been kept apart in separate bottles; the lack of deep cultural traditions, and, consequently, the less complex spiritual structure of the continent; the political and economic setups peculiar to the Americas; the geographical position of the land, open to currents from both the East and the West; the vastness of the territory, with no different intermingled nationalities to rub against each other, and the resultant absence of that pressure which makes for intellectual and spiritual concentration; and, last but not least, the much less accentuated differentiation of social classes.

One further consideration on this matter leads me to refer to the very special case of some of the Latin American republics. I am thinking of those countries in which a rich Indian cultural tradition, supported by a large mass of indigenous people, is still alive. Mexico and Peru are, of course, the most outstanding examples, though by no means the only ones. For years now, an active movement emphasizing what may be called the Indian motif and, in general, the orientation of the national life in the direction of the aboriginal forms of culture, has been afoot in these countries. The social-political and the broader cultural aspects of the matter are interwoven in this movement, as is to be seen in such different manifestations as, for example, the social-political program of the *APRA* group in Peru, as well as in much of the modern literature and art of Mexico.

It would be impossible at this time to say what effect the removal of the pressure of European culture as a consequence of the war may have in this connection, that is to say, whether the result will be the preponderance in these countries of the Euro-American or the Indo-American cultural tradition. That the European tradition should be given up can hardly be imagined and would hardly be possible; but that this tradition will be very substantially modified by an ever-increasing influence of the indigenous Indian tradition is not only possible, but most likely.

In this same connection, I am also inclined to believe that, more even than in the United States, it is in Latin America that the most marked deviations from traditional European culture, as well as perhaps the most original notes of a new American culture, will probably present themselves; and this for several reasons, the most basic of which is the very peculiar racial composition characteristic of the majority of the Latin American countries. As is well known, contrary to what happened in the United States, where the principle of racial purity, at least as far as the white stock is concerned, has prevailed, in Latin America the three main stocks of white, Indian, and Negro have mixed freely, and of this mixture, the quantity and quality of which varies, of course, in each of the different countries, the present Latin American population is to a very large extent the result. In the United States, a lateral influence of the Negro stock—the Indian counting for so little in the life of the country—on the culture of the nation is always possible, and, as a matter of fact, is already very noticeable, especially in popular forms of life, literature, and art. But in

Latin America, owing to the mixture just referred to, this influence, more of the Negro stock in some cases, more of the Indian stock in others, or of both stocks combined, is a constant vertical one permeating the whole of Latin American life from top to bottom—or vice versa. Whether this will by itself give to Latin American life and culture that characteristic of universality which many people think it will, remains, of course, to be seen. What cannot be doubted is that, for good or for bad—for this remains also to be seen,—it will give to the Latin American culture of the future, as, in fact, it has already given to the Latin American culture of the present, a very special and very original character.

This would be the place to discuss the problem of the cultural relations between the United States, on the one hand, and the Latin American countries, on the other, as they are likely to be affected by the war. The problem itself, however, is so complex that I shall have to limit myself to the most fundamental considerations.

That these cultural relations will daily become closer and closer is almost certain. Almost certain it is, also, that the cultural influence of the United States on Latin America will become greater and greater. In the nature of things, this influence should be felt especially in those aspects of culture in which the United States is particularly strong, that is to say, in the fields of science, scientific research, and technical organization and application. In other aspects of culture this influence will have to be, of course, both more limited and more reciprocal; but it will still be important. One can already see evidence of this in the ever-increasing popularity of such leading American literary personalities as Dreiser, Upton Sinclair, Sinclair Lewis, Sherwood Anderson, Hemingway, and O'Neill, among others. Special mention should be made also of the group of writers who, like Waldo Frank, Isaac Goldberg, Carlton Beals, and Anita Brenner, have devoted special and sympathetic attention to Latin America and have greatly helped to improve cultural relations between the two Americas.

It must be remembered in this connection that the final success or failure of the cultural relations will depend on the success or failure of the political-economic relations between the two sections of the continent. The long series of blunders that have characterized practically all the history of the political-economic relations will have to come to an end, if a real improvement is to be expected in so vital an American matter as this. The decision rests, in the end, with the United States. Owing to the efforts of President Roosevelt's administration, much progress has already been made in the right direction, and it is only fair to say that the attitude of Latin America toward the United States is today far more favorable and sympathetic, more confident, in short, than it has ever been.

The idea, itself, of American continental solidarity, nowadays postulated as axiomatic by many people in this country, is to be thought of more as a purpose and a goal than as an actual fact. Historically as well as racially, culturally as well as economically, and, indeed, in part also geographically, Latin America is more closely related to Europe than to the United States. The very political division into nationalities of Latin America, as compared with the political-national unity of the United States, follows in the spirit of European political life. The habit of thinking of Latin America as a unified continental block, rather than as a series of politically independent countries, may be itself a cause of annoying misunderstandings, considering the national susceptibilities of the Latin American countries. A basic course on Latin American geography and history will be of great help to anyone wishing to coöperate in the improvement of political, economic, and cultural relations between the great Republic of the North and the neighboring Republics of the South. The differences between the two sections of the continent being in themselves so many, so great, and so irreducible, the whole matter of cultural relations must be based on the principle of respect for these differences. If this is done, I do not see any reason why these relations should not be as close and as mutually beneficial as could be desired.

I have now discussed what, as I have said, seems to me to be the most significant meaning of the war to the Americas from the cultural viewpoint, namely, the affirmation and definition of American culture as a consequence of the practical suspension of cultural relations between the Old and the New Worlds and the growth of nationalistic feeling resulting from the war.

As a supplement, I wish to speak briefly now of what may be the effect of the war on some of the most important fields of culture, as well as of some of the implications in connection with these various fields.

Specifically, it is my belief that it will be the field of the social sciences that will eventually profit most, in quantity at least, from what I think can be expected to be the stimulating effect of the war. My reason for believing so is the very urgency with which the social problem is pressing on us from all directions—a pressure which, in the nature of things, the war will only help to increase. By the social problem I do not mean only the classic problem of the economic relations between labor and capital; this is but one aspect of the matter. As important, and indeed more important still, are, for example, the social-educational problem of the relation of the rising masses to culture, and the social-spiritual problem of the place of the individual in the complex of the present mass-minded social organization. I mean, in general, the problem of the reshaping of social life in accordance both with the reality of things and the political, economic, educational, and spiritual demands of the times.

Whether we like it or not, it is our fate to live in an age of transition—a transition which, not having come about by way of normal evolution, now threatens to force itself by way of revolution—from an individualistically minded type of social organization like that prevailing during the 19th century to a socially minded one. The problem in the 19th century was how to protect the masses against the abuses of the powerful individual; the problem today begins to be how to protect the humble, modest individual against the pressure and the oppression of the powerful masses, a problem which can perhaps be solved only by protecting the masses against themselves, that is to say, by educating and disciplining them.

My little acquaintance with the problems of the physical

sciences does not allow me to speak with any degree of authority on this matter, but I do not see any reason why this field of knowledge should have to suffer as a result of the war. Aside from the general disruption of cultural life that war always brings with it, it seems to me more likely that certain aspects, at least, of science may profit by the experiences of the war. The same is true of the field of technology. At any rate, as far as the United States is concerned, science and technology, being as advanced as they are, are probably the two fields that will suffer least. My concern in this connection is of a different nature. I am thinking, on the one hand, of the possibility and even the probability that too much emphasis on the technological aspects of science may in the end prove detrimental to the progress of pure science itself. The pressure of the practical, utilitarian motive is a real danger. It may mean that technology also must sooner or later deteriorate for lack of fresh inspiration. And I am thinking, on the other hand, of the already too emphatic tendency to reduce every human problem to the category of a technological problem to be solved by this or that change of method or technique. That every autumn, coinciding more or less with the opening of the academic year, we must have a new model of automobile, is not perhaps in itself so bad; this, however, is no excuse for having also to have a new model of school or college education or a new model of religious believing and praying. There is something both childish and tragic in this hundred-per-cent technological way of looking at life. There is the childish instinct of playing with tools and instruments, methods and techniques, as the child plays with toys. And there is the tragic mechanistic conception that underlies all this technological way of thinking, making of both man and life mere pieces of machinery.

This is, I suppose, the one aspect of culture that will have to be most carefully watched. Entire civilizations have perished for lack of properly developed techniques. Ours, on the other hand, may perish strangled in an excess of techniques. What will have to be especially watched is that man, the machine maker, does not himself become a machine, that is to say, a machine of machines. You cannot build up a sense of moral responsibility when the foundations on which moral responsibility rests have been destroyed. Machines do not obey moral laws, nor human laws either. Only man, when thought of in human terms and so educated, can be expected to obey these laws. The expectation, however, is out of the question when man himself has been reduced to the category of a machine—the "machine man" that our emotional engineers are trying to build up, and of whom Aldous Huxley has drawn a picture in his *Brave New World*. This, and not the innocuous argument that the man of science does not intend his mechanical inventions to be used for criminal purposes, is what must be answered. We already know that man can conquer nature; it remains now to be seen whether he can also conquer himself. On the success or failure of this, the final success or failure of culture will depend.

Optimistic on the whole as I am concerning the fields of the social and physical sciences, I am also extremely skeptical concerning the future of philosophy, literature, and art. I do not mean so much the aspect of historical, scientific research work as the creative aspect in each of these fields. Neither do I mean to imply that a fertile crop of so-called works of philosophy, literature, and art will not be forthcoming, including perhaps some good ones. I am thinking more of the quality than of the quantity, and more in terms of cultural movements than in terms of single works which may appear at any time and under almost any conditions. For the quantity itself may be, and indeed I am inclined to believe will be, large. The same social problems that the social sciences will have to deal with, or similar ones, will naturally suggest themselves as ready raw material for philosophic, literary, and artistic treatment. This is just what, for many years now, has already been happening. The result will, then, be a kind of social, or rather sociological, philosophy, literature, and art. It is only to be questioned what philosophic, literary, and artistic value all this pseudo-literary and pseudo-scientific production may have.

A certain amount, even a great quantity, of war literature and art, that is to say, literature and art dealing with the experience of the war, is naturally to be expected. But perhaps it is also to be expected that the value of this literary and artistic production will be both as sensational and as ephemeral as the value of this kind of literature and art has always been. It is only twenty years since the end of the first World War and the most sensational literary works dealing with that event, such as Blasco Ibáñez's *The Four Horsemen of the Apocalypse,* Barbusse's *Under Fire,* Remarque's *All Quiet on the Western Front,* Hemingway's *A Farewell to Arms,* to mention only a few, are already half forgotten.

My skepticism concerning the future of philosophy, literature, and art is not precisely due to any particular bad effects that the war may have in this respect, but rather to what I think to be the fact that modern life does not offer a favorable atmosphere for philosophic, literary, and artistic creation. The question is not one of lack of techniques, knowledge, or resources; instead, it is the excess of all these things that is in the way. It is the fundamental lack of those conditions of stability, repose, concentration, and detachment from the most pressing practical needs and problems, and above all, of that sense of somewhat permanent values without which philosophy, literature, and art can hardly be expected to prosper. Philosophy, literature, and art are certainly not eternal, but they are conceived in view of some more or less eternal essences or values, and that is, I suppose, their fundamental significance in the work of education. In the whirlwind of men, wills, ideas, problems, tendencies, tastes, standards, and what not, that hustles our modern life, however, the only sense of eternity that seems to be left, on the part of the author as well as of the public, is that of the whirlwind itself. This is the atmosphere in which political, economic, and social programs, plans, and utopias thrive; it certainly is not the atmosphere in which philosophy, literature, and art can breathe.

With this, these remarks come to an end. Knowing how discredited the role of prophet is, I have tried to be as cautious and as conservative as possible in my predictions. There is a most serious difficulty in dealing with a subject which, like that of the meaning of the war to the Americas from the cultural viewpoint, takes us into the future—a difficulty which, not having mentioned it at the beginning of my address, I wish to mention now. We see, of course, in what condition the Old World is today, and, the manner in which the war may come to an end being in itself so uncertain, we realize that any conclusions we may draw concerning the course of future events over there are purely hypothetical. We assume, on the other hand, that, after the war is over, the New World will continue to be the stable reality that it is today. On this assumption many of the foregoing considerations rest. Yet the assumption may prove to be entirely wrong. A German victory, for example, or the total collapse of Europe, might bring about such an internal dislocation in the political, economic, and social aspects of life on the American continent as to change the whole present outlook. What the future of American culture in such a case might be, one can hardly guess.

And this brings me now to my concluding remark. I have had occasion to refer in these pages both to the critical condition of present-day European culture and to the essential solidarity of the European and American branches of Western culture. These are facts not to be forgotten. For it may easily be that Western culture as a whole is in a precarious condition, afflicted by evils which have brought the European branch to the plight in which it finds itself today. For the sake of America and of Western culture, let us hope that the same evils do not affect also the American branch. Let us hope that the solidarity referred to is a solidarity in its assets and not in its liabilities. The fate of the Old World should be a lesson to the New.

www.ingramcontent.com/pod-product-compliance
Lightning Source LLC
Chambersburg PA
CBHW071205240426
43668CB00032B/2099